Antique Memories
TALES FROM A LIFETIME OF COLLECTING ANTIQUES AND FOLK ART

Sonderho Press, Ottawa K0E 1T0
Copyright © 2021, Shaun Markey
All rights reserved. Published 2021.

All photographs used herein are for identification purposes only and are used without the intent to infringe on the owner's proprietary rights. The Acknowledgements section starting on page 201 provides photo credits.

This book is the result of the author's independent research and has been created to provide accurate information concerning the subject matter. Although every precaution has been taken in the preparation of this book, the author and publisher assume no responsibility for errors and omissions.

No portion of this publication may be reproduced or transmitted in any form or by any means, electronic or mechanical, including photography, recording, or any information storage or retrieval system, without permission in writing from the publisher. With approval from the publisher or the author, reviewers may quote brief passages.

Designed and published by Sonderho Press.
Edited by Maria Ford, Phrase Strategy.

Printed in Canada.

ISBN: 978-1-7774267-2-9

This book is printed on acid-free paper.

> Cover photo: That's me arriving back in Ottawa with antiques in the back of my truck. The photo was taken about 1984. My mother in law, the late Edith Cathcart, stands in the background. Edith liked antiques too!

Antique Memories
TALES FROM A LIFETIME OF COLLECTING ANTIQUES AND FOLK ART

SHAUN MARKEY

SONDERHO PRESS

This book is dedicated to Charles Edward Markey, our first grandson who was born May 16, 2021.

Table of Contents

Introduction 1
1. Gold Bond Stamps and the Zen of Collecting 7
2. Antiques and Domestic Negotiation 13
3. Balancing Traditional and Contemporary Folk Art 17
4. Silk Stocking Folk Art, The Grenfell Mission 25
5. Folk Art as "the poor man's Versailles" 33
6. Breaking Up a Collection 43
7. Flea Market Finds 49
8. The Decline of Stories About Antiques in Canadian Media 57
9. Gone Fishin' 65
10. Early Ottawa Antique Dealers, Blake and Ruth McKendry 75
11. Beauty in Wood: Folk Art Masters of the Ottawa Valley 87
12. Memories on Canvas: The Art of Brian Hayes 103
13. The Art of the Chase 111
14. Beyond the Surface: Evaluating Country Furniture 119
15. The Beauty of Small: Salesman's Samples, Children's Furniture,
    and Gifts from the Heart 127
16. A Stroll Through the Woods 135
17. Early Ottawa Antique Dealers, Murray and Mary Copeland 141
18. Visionaries and the Rest of Us 153
19. Good, Better, Best, and Learning to Discern 157
20. Country Furniture of the Ottawa Valley 167
21. Early Ottawa Antique Dealers, Philip and Marge Shackleton 183
22. COVID-19 and the Antique Collector 195
Epilogue 199
Acknowledgements 200
Appendix 1 204
Appendix 2 206
Appendix 3 209
Bibliography 214
Index 218

At home in the man cave in September of 2016. Tony the French Bulldog (now departed) looks on. Photo courtesy of the Ottawa Citizen.

Introduction

As I write this, five years have passed since I wrote *Folk Art in the Attic*. In those five years, the thought of a second book was remote. Joan, and I were busy with life, which, of course, included a significant amount of time looking for antiques and folk art. We made sure to attend the important antique shows each year, took special note of collections that came to auction and regularly attended those events. Road trips out of

Cover of the 2017 calendar produced by the Bytown Antique and Bottle Club to celebrate Canada's 150th birthday.

town, or in town for that matter, were routinely punctuated with stops at antique stores and flea markets.

Once a month, apart from the summer months, I attended evening meetings of the Bytown Antique and Bottle Club and was happily involved in club projects. There was a special calendar we produced for Canada's 150th birthday in 2017 and an impressive display of early Canadian furniture and folk art during our annual show in the same year. All of the items on display were of high quality and contributed by club members.

In 2019, I co-produced and hosted a six-episode television series about antiques and folk art. It was a busy and productive time.

All this activity came to an abrupt halt in mid-March of 2020 when the COVID-19 virus established itself in Canada as an ongoing major health issue.

From that time forward, we did what the authorities instructed us to do, which meant spending a great deal of our time *at home*. Our collecting routines went out the window. Antique shows and auctions were cancelled. Visits to antique shops and flea markets were out of the question. Other than the occasional trip to our cabin in Quebec, road trips and travel also disappeared from our agenda.

For the first six months we busied ourselves with various improvement projects around the house, both inside and out. I spent hours re-organizing the family photo albums. We read books, rearranged furniture, then rearranged the items again. We worked in our front and back gardens and had visits with friends and family there, too. We did a lot of walking around our neighbourhood. Yet, even with all this activity, there were still hours to fill in the days and evenings.

I was sitting at my antique desk in the lower level of our home when the thought of writing a second book crossed my mind. I was quick to dismiss the notion. When the first book was finished and printed, I felt a satisfying feeling of completion. The reviews had been positive and collectors enjoyed it. However, it had been a much bigger project than I anticipated. Writing the manuscript was a challenge but finding photographs, doing the research, conducting interviews, and—constantly, it seemed—reading and rereading the edited manuscript were tasks I was in no hurry to repeat. Besides, the fun part of collecting is collecting, not writing a book on the subject!

A display of museum-quality antique furniture, accessories and folk art at the 2017 Bytown Antique and Bottle Club sale. All items shown from private collections.

Still, thoughts of a second book kept returning. I initially dismissed the idea on the basis that Joan and I had not acquired enough interesting new items in the interim five years. But it slowly occurred to me that the second book could have a different structure from the first. In *Folk Art in the Attic*, each chapter was about a specific acquisition. Since that time, I had accumulated new content in the form of magazine features I had written for trade publications in Canada and the U.S. as well as several other articles and columns that had never seen the light of day. I also had content from several blog posts I had written.

Then, during a telephone conversation, fellow collector Steve Cunliffe mentioned some of the early dealers who operated stores in and around Ottawa. He spoke to me about Blake and Ruth McKendry, Murray and Mary Copeland, and Philip and Marg Shackleton. I was aware of these dealers because they had all written extensively about Canadian antiques and folk art and I had read all their books and many of their articles. But Steve and his wife, Sue Cunliffe, knew them all personally and frequently bought antiques from them. Steve's anecdotes piqued a new interest in me to learn more and write about these early collectors and dealers of Canadian antiques and folk art.

Interviewing Carol Cameron for a segment on textiles and sewing accessories for the television series, Our Antique Treasures 2019, Rogers TV Ottawa.

I corresponded with Jennifer McKendry and Susan Copeland about their parents' careers in antiques and asked if they would be receptive to me writing about them. Their reactions were enthusiastic and both women were generous with anecdotes, information, and photographs.

Bill Dobson, whose stature in the Canadian antiques milieu is as distinguished as those early dealers, encouraged this new project and recounted his own experiences interacting with these early dealers over the years. Based on all this input and the content I had already written, I finally decided to write the book you are holding in your hands.

This book is skewed towards antique country furniture and folk art because that is what Joan and I have collected for forty years. Residing in Ottawa, my exposure is to antiques largely from Eastern Ontario and West Quebec. Notwithstanding the emphasis on country furniture and folk art, I believe my experiences will resonate with any collector, regardless of their specific area of interest.

Why do I collect antiques? Why do my friends and acquaintances collect? These are questions I ask myself frequently. When I was young, I collected comics, marbles, *Hardy Boys* novels, and even the little comics inside of individually wrapped pieces of *Double Bubble* chewing gum. The urge to collect was with me from a young age. My logic went like this: if one object provides personal satisfaction and interest, then another will do the same, and another, and another.

Antique collectors are fascinated with the past and with the objects that were part of people's lives, whether from a hundred years ago, a thousand years ago, or much longer. Each antique reflects the lives of those who came before us. Antique objects provide a glimpse into the past at a human and often emotional level. A 19th-century, chip-carved, oval, splint "bride's box" is an impressive object in its own right, while the care and attention to detail it displays speaks volumes about the affection the maker had for the recipient who received the box as a gift.

Canadian collectors pursue the objects our predecessors used for functional and decorative purposes. When you collect, you bring a small piece of their lives into yours. For collectors, that is powerful social chemistry.

"When you collect, you bring a small piece of the original owners' lives into yours. For collectors, that is powerful social chemistry."

I have tried to be as accurate as possible in describing the early days of antiquing in Ottawa with additional references to antique dealers in Ontario, Quebec, Nova Scotia, and the U.S. Undoubtedly there are errors, but I hope they are minimal. I am happy to revise the digital version of the book and those changes will be reflected in future printings.

So, this is the book that I thought I would never write. This is my pandemic project.

I hope you enjoy reading about the early days of antiques in Ottawa, my personal antique adventures, and, occasionally, my misadventures. The discoveries, pursuits, and acquisition of special antiques and folk art are terrific experiences. I wish the same for you.

Ottawa, Ontario
February 8, 2021

Future Gold Bond Stamps collector at my first communion in 1957. I am the snappy dresser in the double breasted jacket and short pants! Brothers Stephen on the left, brother Scott on right. Sister Sharon on the right. Mum and Dad (Rita and Edward Markey) behind.

Gold Bond Stamps and the Zen of Collecting

The urge to collect has been with me practically my entire life. How did it start? Why does "collecting" objects, in my case folk art and antiques, continue to preoccupy me decades after I turned my attention to the pastime?

Perhaps I got the collecting bug as a young boy, when my mother collected *Gold Bond Stamps* at our local IGA grocery store on Merivale Road, at the time on the outskirts of Ottawa. Back in the 1950s and '60s, she would fill the trunk of the car with purchases for a family of eight, nine if you include my grandmother who lived with us for some thirty years.

Back then, $100 filled the massive trunk of our '66 Meteor almost completely. It took

The Gold Bond Stamps booklet.

a steady progression of my brothers and sister to march all those full paper grocery bags into the kitchen of our suburban Ottawa home. Last week, I spent $100 at the grocery store and the entire haul fit neatly into a small basket I carried with one hand!

After each shopping trip, we received the precious Gold Bond Stamps, distributed based on the volume of groceries purchased, then carefully and dutifully glued them into a corresponding booklet. The Gold Bond Stamp books would steadily increase in thickness and the trove was kept in a drawer to the right of the refrigerator. I remember watching them expand in number until it became difficult to shut the drawer.

At a certain point, after much begging and cajoling by us, my mother would declare that we had reached the required number of books. We children would have exchanged them far earlier but, when it came to the maturity of Gold Bond Stamps, Mum was steadfast, holding out against the pleas of her six children until only she felt the time was right!

Finally, much discussion and review of the *Gold Bond Catalogue* would ensue: for which piece of merchandise would those precious stamp books be redeemed? Once the new toaster, iron, or hair dryer was home, the whole process started again.

Or perhaps my passion for collecting began because of the games of marbles we used to play at recess and lunch hour in the schoolyard. The most impressive storage container for one's marbles was the dark-purple velvet bags inside the boxes in which Seagram's Crown Royal whiskey was sold.

These sturdy bags with their gold-coloured draw-string and stitching kept the marbles safe and nicely transportable until the next game, when each of us tried to roll one marble at a time into the "pot", a depression that someone in the group would prepare by slamming the heel of their shoe into the dirt then turning in a circle to create a shallow hole in the earth. Of course, the smaller the depression was, the more difficult the challenge of rolling our precious marbles into it.

The players would retreat to about fifteen feet from the pot, crouch, then use the flat edge of the forefinger to project the marble toward the pot. The first person to successfully get their marble into the pot won. Sometimes, it took a lot of marbles before someone claimed the prize: all the marbles that had missed and lay around the pot.

The six gallon butter churn Joan and I found on my ancestors' farm. It was partially restored by Rita Markey in 1982.

I recall a day when I won a massive pot of marbles. It included several of the larger, much-prized "boulders", which one player foolishly opted to use after he had exhausted his supply of regular-sized marbles. Ah, to the winner go the spoils! In this case, however, it took me several minutes after the sound of the bell beckoning us to class to gather up all the marbles, including stuffing the overflow into my pant pockets. Several pounds of marbles in my front pockets gave me thighs that looked like a football running back and made a distinct clacking sound as I rushed into class several minutes late.

For the rest of the afternoon, I made occasional adjustments to my load, so to speak, to keep the ballast evenly distributed and not fall out of my chair. Getting home on my bike after school was a wobbly challenge, too!

I also collected the little sheets of comics that came inside gum wrappers. Later, I graduated to full-size comics. *Archie* was one of my favourite titles. It was exciting to acquire a new issue and follow the adventures of *Archie* and his friends, Veronica, Betty, Reggie, and Jughead Jones. Hockey and football cards came next.

My passion for collecting abated in high school and college, perhaps due to a meager income, only to resurface with a vengeance when I started my career. Research into my family history and finding artifacts like the pieces of an old six-gallon stoneware butter churn buried on the site of my ancestral farm inspired Joan and I to start collecting antique country furniture and accessories. On one of our first dates, we attended an auction in the village of Finch, Ontario, about thirty-five miles southeast of Ottawa. We watched in fascination as dusty, antique pine furniture sold for hundreds of dollars. The auctioneer sold small items from the porch on the back of the little frame house and these items, too, brought what seemed to us to be extraordinary amounts of money. From that day on, attending auctions became one of our regular activities.

Today, I have several decades of antique and folk art collecting behind me. I have, it occurs to me, much more of a collecting past than a future, yet still the excitement of a new find makes my adrenaline rush as strongly as ever. Discovering and restoring an antique cupboard or harvest table that has been relegated to a basement or out-building for storing old cans, bottles, and tools is not only a thrill but also gives the satisfaction of saving a piece of cultural history.

2
Antiques and Domestic Negotiation

Tension arises in our house about the interior display of the antiques and folk art we collect. Joan is a "less is more" type. She believes a small number of antique or decorative items in a room heighten their visual impact. I am a "more is more" type. I like many objects in a room, the busier the better. I like looking at the objects we have collected because there is a story behind every one of them.

Even with her "less is more" interior design maxim, Joan likes to change things up, so several times a year, I find myself subcontracted to rearrange furniture in the various living spaces in our home. Often, to no one's surprise, this

Surrounded with antiques and folk art in the man cave!

process produces a net surplus of items, which are moved to the man-cave in the basement, our default repository for victims of the culling. It almost happened again this past weekend, but I somehow managed to rearrange the antiques and art in the family room without losing anything to the man cave. The dialogue went something like this:

"Joanie, don't you think an antique cupboard at each of the sofa looks so, well, *symmetrical?*" My eyebrows arched hopefully upwards as I waited for a reply. "They're sort of like bookends," I added confidently.

Joan returned a withering glance, but on this occasion, she relented, and for now, two antique cupboards pleasingly bookend our sofa.

Innocent collectors must be warned of the "let's paint the house" threat to a collection. A friend of mine agreed with his partner to paint the interior of their home, which of course necessitates moving out the antiques and furniture. Once finished, he had a devil of a time convincing his partner to return the antiques back to their original places. I am always on guard against the "let's paint the house" ruse.

Unless you are collecting postage stamps or other dimensionally un-challenged collectibles, at some point you are going to run out of space. Either that, or you stop collecting, an unacceptable solution for most of us. Some folks collect furniture and art to the

More is more in action. 2020.

point that every room in their house is rather full. The rationale is: why stop something that is interesting and fun to do? Besides, if one stops acquiring, what would there be to talk about with one's buddies at the antique market?

If you live in a rural setting with barns or enough land to build out-buildings, you are indeed fortunate. However, even barn-blessed collectors run out of space. I know some who have filled their available buildings to the eaves. Is it any wonder there are so many of those commercial storage facilities popping up all over the place?

Like it or not, the collector's day of reckoning will come. In my case, with six antique pine cupboards in the house and two in the garage, any new cupboard acquisition would have to be a jaw-dropper to make its way into the collection. The same goes for blanket boxes, of which we have several. Of lamp tables, we have an easy half-dozen or more. Tables: a harvest type, two round ones, and another cut-down (I did not do it!) harvest-type that serves as a coffee table, plus various washstands, servers, pedestal tables, bucket benches, and more. I have not even mentioned the folk art sculpture and paintings on the walls.

Although our supply of antiques has dropped off in recent years, I still see pieces in the backs of picker's trucks and in shops that make me swoon.

In the man-cave, I let loose. There, I stack, arrange, fill, and shelve as many objects as I like. Although I have achieved "detente" in the man-cave, there are no signed documents or treaties, so, like a small country in the shadow of a superpower, I live with the uncertainty that Joan may have a change of heart and set her "less is more" sights on the lower level of our home. Until that day comes, however, like a squirrel urgently building a nest in the garden shed, I live in happy bliss surrounded by antiques and folk art.

Wood carving of moose by Abe Patterson 1950's, Private collection.

3
Balancing Traditional and Contemporary Folk Art

Early dealers of country furniture and folk art did not buy or sell contemporary pieces. Their preference was to search out traditional folk art—items dating back into the 19th century and preferably long before that. Many dealers and collectors will not embrace contemporary folk art. In their minds, it does not have the quality and history that age brings to a piece. It is hard to argue with that logic; however, contemporary folk art has become increasingly popular over the years. It is widely collected and commands impressive prices at auctions. Contemporary folk art is also easier to find than traditional folk art, and in most cases is less expensive.

Artistic expression is crucial with folk art. That factor combined with form, condition, age, colour, and provenance all contribute to the allure of an item.

Crucifix wood carving by Arthur Sauvé mid 1950s. Private collection.

Folk art gives a glimpse into the life of people who came before us, those who settled this country and modestly decorated their surroundings to reflect the immediate world around them. Folk art often depicts religious or spiritual themes. Crucifix subjects, church gatherings, angels, and more are often subjects depicted in folk art carvings, paintings, and textiles.

I like this definition of folk art from well-respected collector, Dr. Alvin "Nick" Cameron:

> "Folk art is the untrained embellishment of a utilitarian object whose function is in no way enhanced by the embellishment. The creation is a personal, individual visual experience, possibly unique that 'pleases the eye' of both creator and beholder, never intended for resale, usually intended as a one-time-only creation, naïvely done, by an individual untrained in the rules of art, often meant as a gift."

Nick's definition touches on the key aspects of folk art: pieces often have a naïve appearance, are unique, and are created by individuals untrained in the rules of art. His point about "embellishment of a utilitarian object" is a good one, too. Individuals in 19th-century Canada often added artistic features to an otherwise common object, thereby elevating its appearance. These characteristics are especially true of traditional folk art and collectors are always looking for these objects.

Regarding traditional versus contemporary folk art, Nick's distinction is important: traditional pieces were "never intended for resale", whereas contemporary folk art is frequently offered for sale, either by the artist or by someone who buys the items directly from the artist then re-offers them for sale.

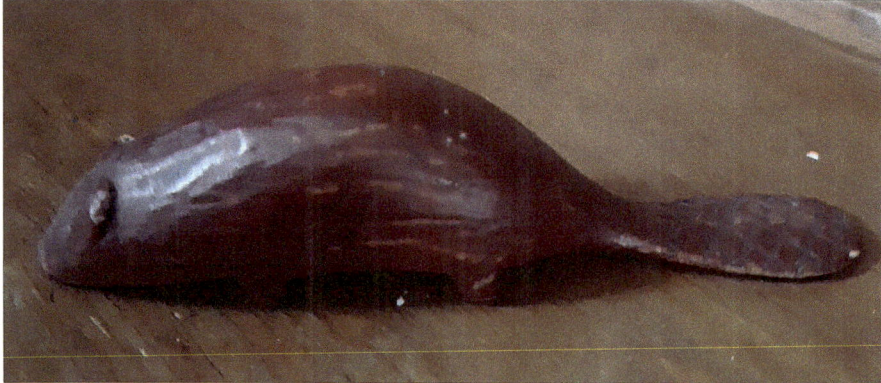

Exquisite small wood carving of a beaver by Howard Sarazin, Calumet Island, Quebec, 1910. Private collection.

However, the distinction is not black-and-white. Most folk artists do sell their art while they are alive, and the confirmation that their art has monetary value may encourage some to produce more and more works. In some cases, the innocence of the work can be compromised when the art is promoted and moves into the commercial marketplace.

On the other hand, many contemporary folk artists are not interested in selling their work. I have seen entire houses filled with the owner's own folk art paintings. In one case, I made an offer on a painting at a man's house in Brockville but the artist could not bring himself to sell even one of them although he had dozens hanging on the walls in every room.

Renowned folk artists like Maud Lewis, Joe Norris, Joe Sleep, and many others all sold their artwork. Joe Sleep (1914–1978), for example, was acutely aware of the market for his works. Like other folk artists, he used stencils and cut-outs to increase his output. He painted on small panels that would fit in a tourist's suitcase. If a particular subject did not sell, he stopped painting it. Sales of his artwork represented an important source of income during the few years that he painted in the mid to late 1970s.

Sales of her paintings were an important source of income for Maud Lewis

Painting of a cat with butterfly and flowers, by Joe Sleep. Author's collection.

(1900–1970) of Marshalltown, Nova Scotia. She, too, was aware of what her customers wanted, repeated many of the same scenes, and used stencils. I have a copy of a letter she wrote to one of her customers in the early 1960s apologizing for the delay in responding to a request for a particular painting. In her letter, she notes that she had over 300 requests for paintings at the time!

Painting by Maud Lewis, early 1960s. Author's collection.

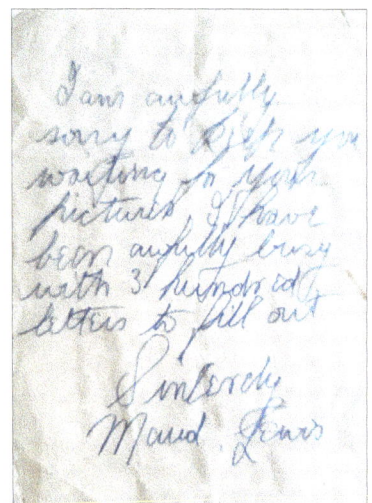

Note written to a customer by Maud Lewis early 1960s. Author's collection.

In their book, *'Twas Ever Thus*, Dr. Ralph Price and Patricia Price include in the Foreword a classification system for folk art. The system, originally devised by Louis C. and Agnes Hasey Jones of the New York State Historical Association at Cooperstown, attempts to organize folk art "into a manageable whole".

In the model, traditional folk art— including sculpture, paintings, quilts, samplers, hooked rugs, decoys, toys, ceramics trade signs, and other individually created work—is placed in a circle in the middle. What they call "associative folk art" or "directed work" is placed in an outer circle. Items in the outer circle include products of cottage industries, like trade figures, figure heads, or work which is close to a Craft Tradition, including feather and hair wreaths, hooked rugs, samplers, paintings after prints, and ethnic art.

The late Dr. Ralph Price and Patricia Price, authors of 'Twas Ever Thus, 1979.

> *"The essence is the difference between individual work and that which has been supervised; the individual, hand carved decoy as opposed to the factory version."*
>
> – Ralph and Patricia Price

The Prices emphasize: "Personally, we accept them all as folk art, accept them all as valid folk art expressions," and go on to specify: "The essence is the difference between individual work and that which has been supervised; the individual, hand carved decoy as opposed to the factory version." Using the circle model then, hooked mats from Grenfell industries and the studios of George Edward Tremblay, to use two examples, can be placed in the "associative folk art" category in the outer circle.

All folk artists are unknown until such time as someone discovers their work. Since many folk artists decorate their houses and yards with their art, it is not long before neighbours, tourists, and antique pickers notice the art and want to buy it.

On the few occasions when I have come across an unknown folk artist with a home or yard filled with their art, the artist thought their creations had no commercial value. Yet in some cases, the person who discovers their art offers to buy one or two pieces and from that first sale a business relationship is born.

In the early 1980s, we lived in Pembroke, Ontario and I spent most of my Saturday mornings going to yard sales and auctions. I met Art Dixon (1917–2011) at one of these, although I do not recall the exact circumstances. It is possible he was having a yard sale and I stopped to look at the items for sale, which included some vibrantly painted pieces of folk art. I do remember talking to this quiet and gentle man about those pieces, and before long he invited me into his basement workshop to view the other items he had created.

Art's basement was full of wonderful wood carvings all made by him. To my surprise, I discovered he had never sold a piece of his art. I was taken by his work, which ranged from small letter openers with carved birds incorporated into the handle to much larger pieces, some four feet in height, of lumberjacks and other characters. His pieces had a naïve charm and were all brightly painted. I bought several items that day and still own some of them.

Discovering a new artist is just one of the potential thrills of collecting contemporary folk art, which opens up all kinds of possibilities. However, there are some important considerations, the first of which is knowing the difference between tra-

Painted wood carving of a singing lumberjack, by Art Dixon. early 1980s. Author's collection.

ditional and contemporary work, then deciding whether you will collect folk art that has been created up to the present day.

As previously noted, traditional folk art is much older than contemporary folk art. It is often antique (made 100 years ago or more), although that time frame is flexible. Personally, I stop well short of pieces made in the last twenty-five years, although that is an arbitrary decision on my part. I prefer folk art that has some age. On that basis, I will add items to our collection that were made in the 1960s and 1970s, but an object younger than that would have to be truly exceptional to make the cut.

In their splendid book, *Folk Art in Canada*, Michael Rowan and John Fleming chose a demarcation point of 1950 to determine where traditional Canadian folk art ends and contemporary Canadian folk art begins. All the items in their publication were made prior to 1950, with the majority dating to the 19th century. In another book on the subject, *Spirit of Nova Scotia* by Richard Henning Field, the author selects 1930 as the cut-off date for items he includes.

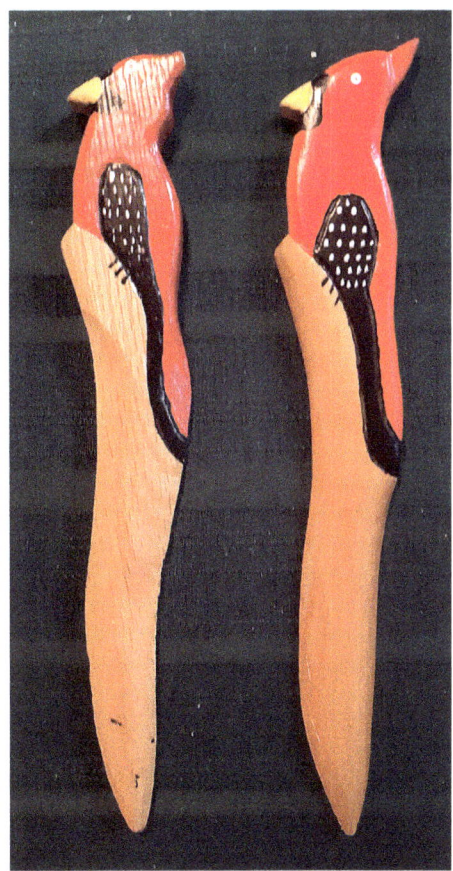

Letter opener, by Art Dixon. Early 1980s. Author's collection.

Just as important as age is knowing what truly is folk art and what is not. Ultimately, it is your collection so you will decide the constraints and limits under which you will operate. Let your knowledge, experience, understanding, and personal taste guide you to build a folk art collection to enjoy for many years.

Polar bear on ice flow, Grenfell Mission, Private collection.

4
Silk Stocking Folk Art, The Grenfell Mission

As a collector and sometime dealer in country furniture and folk art, my radar is always tuned for good hooked mats, especially those made by the Grenfell Mission. Like most collectors and dealers, I find much to admire about these finely crafted mats. They were made primarily from donated silk stockings and produced by women in remote outports of Newfoundland and Labrador on Canada's east coast, starting about 1930. It has been my good fortune over the years to find and purchase several of them.

The Grenfell Mission was established in 1892 in Labrador and the Great Northern Peninsula of Newfoundland by Dr. Wilfred Grenfell (1865–1940), a British doctor and medical missionary from Parkgate, England. At the time of its founding, the Dominion of

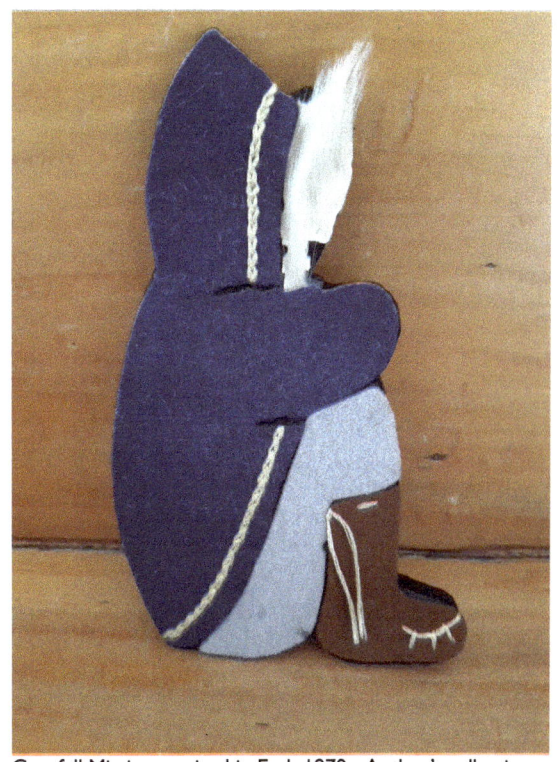

Grenfell Mission sewing kit. Early 1970s. Author's collection.

Newfoundland was an isolated British colony and would not become the Canadian province of Newfoundland and Labrador until 1949.

The province of Newfoundland and Labrador today is without question one of the most fascinating places to visit in North America. When Dr. Grenfell first visited there in 1892, at the age of twenty-seven, he was already experienced in attending to the medical needs of fishermen in the North Sea because of a three-year stint on medical ships dedicated to that purpose. In Canada, he discovered the bleak living conditions of the inhabitants of Labrador and northern Newfoundland predominantly indigenous peoples and British immigrants.

Dr. Wilfred Grenfell, founder of the Grenfell Mission. Photo courtesy of Grenfell Historic Properties.

On that first trip, he travelled the coast, administering to the medical needs of the residents. The population was a meager 5,000 people widely scattered about a huge area of 110,000 square miles—and without a single doctor. After that first experience, Dr. Grenfell decided to make his life's work helping the humble and hardworking people of Labrador and northern Newfoundland.

Although its mandate was the provision of medical services, Dr. Grenfell's mission went on to create and maintain five hospitals, four nursing stations, an orphanage, two large boarding schools, two hospital ships, several smaller boats, and numerous cooperatives, clothing stores, and industrial centres.

Dr. Grenfell was convinced that the people under his care needed more than medical help. Led by the New England artist, Jessie Luther (1860–1952), whom Dr. Grenfell recruited in 1906, a weaving cottage-industry was successfully introduced and developed, followed by the hooked mat enterprise beginning in 1908. The remote northern environment in which Grenfell mats were made undoubtedly inspired much of their charm and appeal, which manifests in finely executed "far north" images and scenes. Dr. Grenfell apparently created several of the early designs himself.

Although they were produced in volume, textile products from Grenfell Industries, especially early examples, are difficult to find. Textiles, like hooked mats, are notoriously fragile. Left exposed to the sun, their colours fade. Left on the floor, they can be quickly damaged by foot traffic and stains. Repairing these items can be expensive and requires an experienced hand to match the hooking and colours.

Province of Newfoundland Labrador, Grenfell Industries, early 1960s. Author's collection.

Several years ago, as I was reviewing the listing for a local auction, one item caught my eye: a hooked mat featuring the image of a sailboat with mountains in the background. The short description called it a "tapestry" but as soon as I saw the image, I was certain it was a Grenfell Mission product. Grenfell mats typically have images of the far north featuring wildlife, dark borders, beautiful colours, and tight hooking.

The auction was scheduled for Sunday morning and I made sure to attend the preview. After one walk through the hall and not finding the mat, I asked a staff member for help. She walked me back to the front of the hall and pointed to the mat the rug lying on a table entirely covered by a set of dishes. It was no wonder I had missed it.

Moving some of the dishes and plates to get a better view of the mat, I was immediately struck by its size—a whopping 54" by 32". It featured an ocean landscape with a two-masted sailboat gliding on the current, the forward sails filled with wind, and mountains profiled in the background.

Carefully, I turned back each corner to see whether the tell-tale Grenfell Mission label was on the underside. The Mission had seven different labels, which were used through the 1950s. In this case there was no label, which was not surprising, as they often detach either through wear and tear or because an owner removes them.

Still, I was not deterred. The mat had the tight, densely hooked form common to Grenfell Mission products. The colors were bright and nicely contrasted. It had a double border, including the very dark brown one commonly seen on Grenfell mats. Label or no label, I was convinced it was the real thing.

The reverse side of the sailboat mat by Grenfell Industries, mid 1980s. Private collection.

Despite the sluggish economy, the market for Grenfell mats remains strong, although not as strong as it once was. I bought my first mat in 1989, "Vertical Bear", and had little trouble selling it at the Ashbury College Antique Show for $1,600. It was a large example featuring a polar bear on an ice flow. I have recently seen "Dog Team with Shadows", a dyed silk and rayon beauty designed by Stephen Hamilton in 1942, at an antique show priced at $5,000.

Because Grenfell mats remain popular with collectors, many rugs are wrongly attributed to the Mission. A Grenfell attribution can add hundreds of dollars to the asking price of a mat, and collectors should be cautious.

I was not able to stay for the auction, so I left a bid with a friend and went about the rest of my day. Later that afternoon, my doorbell rang and my friend was standing on the doorstep with the rug under his arm.

We laid it out in the living room to have a good look. After studying the rug for several minutes, I believed my instincts and initial thoughts about it were correct: this was a genuine Grenfell rug, and I was pleased to have acquired it.

"I started doing shows in the States in 1982 and this was where I would find most of the Grenfell items that I was excited to purchase and bring back to Canada and place them in Canadian collections."

— Carol Telfer

I contacted Carol Telfer, of Carol Telfer Antiques, for a second opinion on the mat. She specializes in antique textiles and has extensive knowledge of mats from Grenfell Industries. I described the mat as best I could and sent her a photo. As always, Carol provided helpful information and pointed out, embarrassingly for me, that I had sent her a photo of the back of the mat, not the front! Carol wrote:

> "Hi Shaun: Looks like you have a picture of the back of the mat. It is a Grenfell mat but it was not made during the 'Grenfell period', meaning during Grenfell's life (died in 1940). In 1983 they re-established the mission under the 'Handicraft' label. This mat has all the characteristics of a mat around this period. (Probably why the label was removed). This does not mean that they aren't collectible as they are…….a slight difference in value though."

My experience with that mat is an example of a lesson well learned over years of collecting: a little knowledge is a dangerous thing! I can spot a Wilfrid Richard carving from ten feet away, but apparently, at least in this particular instance, could not tell the front from the back of a Grenfell mat when I am six inches from it!

Carol, on the other hand, has a great deal of knowledge on the subject based on years of experience and study:

> "In my search and growing interest with hooked rugs and quilts, the Grenfell mats captured my attention because of the history they represented coming from such a remote part of Canada. I was immediately attracted to the numerous varieties of depictions portraying life in Newfoundland and Labrador as well as the precise technique in the hooking of the mats—the dyes used in creating outstanding colour—and later the rare and unusual geometric designs introduced to the Industrial through designers hired by Dr. Grenfell after the Mission was well established. I started doing shows in the States in 1982 and this was where I would find most of the Grenfell items that I was excited to purchase and bring back to Canada and place them in Canadian collections. Robin Moore was one of my best collectors during this period but there were others as well—The Miller Carmichael Collection (Quebec) is also very noteworthy. Grenfell mats and artifacts grew in popularity over the years with collectors in Canada, the USA and also in England. They are as popular now as they were back in the '80s—[they are] really the one textile that hasn't been affected by the fluctuation of the marketplace. This is such a reward for the work and diligence of the Canadian and U.S. dealers throughout these past 40 plus years as these dealers continue to promote the importance of this unique art."

The story of my Grenfell mat does not end there. Being somewhat disappointed with the mat, given its later date of creation, I decided to sell it to a fellow collector/dealer for about what I paid for it. He promptly posted the mat on the Internet and sold it for quite a bit more than what he paid me. That brings me to another lesson I learned late in my collecting life: do not lose confidence in the good items you buy.

I have been asked whether I consider Grenfell mats to be folk art. After reading the Prices' book on folk art and learning of the "two-circle" classification system for folk art, I believe they are. Specifically, Grenfell rugs fall within a category the Prices call associative folk art; that is, folk art that is made in a "directed" setting, such as a cottage industry. By con-

A superlative Grenfell Industries mat. Private collection.

trast, a piece of folk art created solely by an individual would fall in the primary category.

Aside from the quality and artistic merit of Grenfell rugs, every one of them is a testament to the work and the mission of Dr. Grenfell and his team. Each Grenfell mat is a legacy, a reflection of the unyielding spirit and heartiness of the individuals who hand-crafted them by the flickering light of an oil lamp in the remote communities of Newfoundland and Labrador.

Dominique Lavallée, active 1977 to 1990, grandson of Wilfrid Richard, is thought to have carved the large otter and possibly the dog as well. Several other members of the extended Richard family were excellent carvers.

5

Folk Art as "The Poor Man's Versailles"

The characteristics I most admire about collectors and dealers are their passion for antiques and the willingness to put that passion (and their bank accounts) to the test to obtain exceptional pieces of Canadian material history. Long-time collector and dealer, Larry Foster, once said to me: "If I like an object and I have the money, I always buy it."

I frequently spend much time and energy debating the purchase of a particular antique—a tendency that only becomes stronger as the cost of an item increases. Is it worth the money? Is there enough quality in the piece? Is there enough money left in it should I decide to sell? After much over-thinking, the decision to not buy an object is often the outcome, despite your initial attraction to it.

This is a story of one collector/dealer and the strength of his convictions about buying Canadian antiques and folk art.

This story began for me in 2020, when I read an article by Richard Field in the 1980 July/August back-issue of *Canadian Antiques and Art Review*. Field covered the venerable Bowmanville Antique Show of that same year and highlighted a special exhibit in which participating dealer, Sam Stuart, dedicated his entire booth to 145 pieces of folk art by the Beardmore, Ontario artist, Ewald Renz (1907–1995). The article states that the collection was discovered by Mr. Stuart's brother-in-law, Herb Gray, north of Thunder Bay, Ontario.

Mr. Rentz carved largely "as-found" pieces of wood—pieces in which the form of the wood often suggests the subject matter. Mr. Stuart was offering the entire collection as one set. Field's article explains that the

$33,000 asking price was established to give the Centre for Canadian Folk Cultural Studies, a division of the then-named National Museum of Man in Ottawa, an opportunity to buy the collection. For various reasons, the Centre declined.

Folk artist, Ewald Rentz (1908–1985).

Despite repeated requests to break up the collection, Mr. Stuart stood his ground and the show continued that weekend with the Rentz collection being offered whole.

One man had seen the collection on the Friday opening night and lost sleep over it. He debated with himself long and hard about purchasing the Rentz collection. By morning Claude Arsenault, then a Toronto-based antique and folk art dealer with a small shop on Scollard Street, had made his decision. He returned to the show the next day and bought the entire collection at the asking price.

In today's market, carvings by Ewald Rentz are extremely popular with folk art collectors. Prices for individual pieces of his work range from $275 to over $2,000. But, at the time of the Bowmanville show in 1980, he had been only recently discovered.

As I read the article, the name, Claude Arsenault, was familiar. Through Facebook groups devoted to Canadian antiques and folk art, I had met (virtually) a Claude Henry Arsenault who was a retired collector/dealer living in Prince Edward Island. Over the previous several years, he had posted fascinating and wonderful photos of an 18th-century house in PEI, called The Lyle House, a one and one-half storey, single-gable Georgian residence with Greek revival details which he had carefully restored to its original condition. He also posted photos of his restoration work on several impressive pieces of early country furniture, which he used to decorate the period home.

After reading the article, I wondered if it could be the same person and decided to ask him. Using Facebook Messenger, I sent Claude a short note describing the article I had read in the magazine and asked if he was the dealer at the Bowmanville show in 1980 who purchased the Ewald Rentz collection.

Within minutes, he responded: "Yes."

We continued a long and lively exchange about the Rentz collection and Claude's career as a dealer in folk art in Toronto. He opened his store, called Home Again, in 1976 with his then-partner, Louis de Niverville (1933–2019). Claude believes Home Again was the first gallery in Canada to specialize in Canadian contemporary folk art, and he featured the entire Rentz collection there in the fall of 1980. The Rentz pieces proved to be popular with Canadian and American collectors and every item sold.

Cover of Home Again Gallery's brochure for their Rentz sale.

Claude continued to operate his Toronto gallery until 1982, during which time he carried the work of many artists who would go on to become veritable icons of Canadian folk art. For example, Claude was one of the first persons to buy the work of Edmond Chatigny (1895–1992) from St. Isidore de Beauce, Quebec. Mr. Chatigny was known for his wildly painted carvings of birds and animals, often using one bird carving as a base platform upon which he would mount several other smaller birds.

Works by Mr. Chatigny rarely come to market. However, a recent auction of a portion of the collection of Dr. Martin Osler by Miller and Miller Auctions clearly demonstrated that demand for his work remains strong. One of the most successful lots in the sale was an impressive Chatigny carving, described in the catalogue as a "monumental birds sculpture," which soared to a final hammer price of $7,000. Other smaller but still impressive, Chatigny works in the same sale ranged in price from $1,100 to $2,500.

Folk art sculptures by Edmond Chatigny in the Home Again folk art gallery, 1980. Private collection.

Claude also became friends with Wilfrid Richard and purchased many works from this masterful Quebec folk artist. He bought and sold the work of many other Quebec folk artists, including Felicien Levesque, Hosanna Dupuis, Alcide St. Germaine, Georges Desmeules, and others. In his gallery, he also featured works by folk artists of Atlantic Canada, including pieces from Charlie Tanner and Sydney Howard.

Carving of a duck boat with hunter and twenty-one miniature decoys, by Charlie Tanner, mid 1970s. Private collection.

Among his favourite folk art items was a life-size carving of a dog, a boxer breed, by Wilfrid Richard. He said that Mr. Richard carved several life-sized pieces.

Life-size painted wood carving of a dog, by Wilfrid Richard. Mid 1970's.

Claude Arsenault, centre, with Mr. and Mrs. Richard, about 1975. Photo courtesy of C. Arsenault.

By 1982, however, Claude had become disillusioned with Canadian folk art. More and more dealers were carrying and aggressively promoting it and folk art had become, Claude thought, a commodity. As a result, he closed his gallery.

Today, judging from his email replies, Claude's convictions about the genre remain strong. In one of his messages to me, Claude wrote of the folk artists he knew in the 1970s: "Stumbling upon these people was like a dream, to see their world, their creative souls, making yard art, like a poor man's Versailles!"

Painted wood carving of a white rabbit, by Wilfrid Richard. Late 1970's. Author's collection.

According to David Lambert, son of Robert Lambert (1933–2007) and Nancy Lambert (1935–1975), The *April Antiques & Folk Art Show*, as originally named, was founded by his mother in 1973 and held at the *Flying Dutchman Motor Inn* in Bowmanville, Ontario. He also said that his father didn't think mounting an antique show was a good idea at the time, but Nancy persisted.

Around the same time, the Lamberts produced a book together titled, *An Historical Sketch of Tyrone*, referring to the little village near Bowmanville where they lived in a log home. Nancy wrote the text and Rob did the sketches. The little book and his mother's interest in antiques prompted her idea to organize an antique show.

In a message to me, David wrote: "She was the reason we got into antiques back when Dad was building our log house. She would go to the *Haydon Auction* barn where good old Cliff Pethic was the auctioneer and buy this old junky furniture to furnish the house with and it all snowballed from there!"

David also explained that the show's logo, the winged cherub, still in use to this day, was designed by his father.

The first promotional brochure was designed by family friend, Mel Shakespeare, and mailed to 1,500 potential buyers. The brochure included this touching tribute to Nancy: "The quality of content shown in this catalogue is due to the keen, unfailing effort of Nancy Lambert. She had the ability to bring out the best in all of us. This will always be her show."

Front cover of the first April Antiques and Folk Art Show.

An array of antique tables from the collection of Reider Olsen. 2019. Photo courtesy of Finer Things Antiques, Halifax, NS.

6
Breaking Up a Collection

At some point, most collectors are confronted with the prospect of breaking up a collection. Some choose to sell *en masse* to a dealer or group of dealers. Others consign their collections, either in a large, one-time sale or a series of auctions. Some collectors choose to donate or sell their cherished antiques and art to a museum, which keeps the collection together—an important consideration to the collector who spent precious time and money gathering the pieces in the first place. The downside of donating a collection is that it removes its contents from the market essentially forever. Donated collections are also rarely seen in a public exhibit and frequently are left in storage for years or decades until the institution has the resources to mount an exhibit.

Curating a major exhibit of antiques is an expensive undertaking and even national cultural institutions have limited resources or need underwriting for the costs from corporations or other wealthy organizations. Without funding for curated exhibitions, archived items can, at best, be made available for scholarly research and study.

Museums and galleries often sell objects from existing collections to finance new acquisitions. This strategy can backfire, often with embarrassing publicity. If there is a weak silver lining to these incidents, it is that a cultural institution and their financial difficulties receive attention in the media.

Buying privately or at auction are both excellent ways to improve a collection. The pieces you buy may not be fresh to the market, but they do come with the provenance of being owned by the previous collector, giving the antiques added status and firmly establishing their authenticity.

About five years ago, my good friend of 40 years, dealer Rick Huxtable, received a call from a collector who lived in a small red brick house just a two-minute walk from the Rideau Canal in Ottawa South. Her circa-1910 row house was crammed with colourful pieces of folk art, primarily from Quebec, which she had decided to sell in anticipation of a move to a different Canadian city. Rick made the visit and came away with several pieces, including examples by Wilfrid Richard. He put the carvings on display in his booth in the Ottawa Antique Market, which I happened to visit the next day.

Wilfrid Richard (1894–1996) is one of the most collectible and talented of all Canadian folk artists. His father, Damasse Richard was a brilliant wood carver as were other members of the extended Richard family. Like the creations of Mr. Richard senior, Wilfrid Richard's carvings of domestic and wild animals exhibit a charming naïveté that places them at the highest level of Canadian folk art. At the time, I was unfamiliar with this artist whose carvings are, understandably, found primarily in Quebec. I was immediately impressed and bought a Richard carving of a hen from Rick that day. At home, I placed it on the fireplace mantle and studied it more closely, the quality appealing to me more and more with each glance.

Wood carving of a hen, by Wilfrid Richard. Early 1980s. Author's collection.

The next day, I hustled back to the antique market to see if I could buy the other Richard carvings that I had seen in Rick's booth. Alas, I was too late! Another collector had bought them all. Then, Rick did something that rarely happens in the antique field: he handed me a small piece of paper with the name and phone number of the original collector and encouraged me to call or stop by her home near the canal, as there were still many pieces of folk art she wanted to sell. Since her home was only a few blocks away, I drove right there.

A few minutes later, I was at her door and she welcomed me into her charming home, which was chock-full of folk art. By the end of my visit, I had acquired fifteen or twenty folk art items plus two small pieces of furniture. Many more desirable pieces remained that I did not buy. Those objects, along with furniture, paintings, and accessories, were destined for a tag sale the following weekend.

A pair of carved painted goats by Wilfrid Richard. Mid 1970s. Author's collection.

Since my acquisition of the Richard carvings, I've learned more about Quebec folk art. It's a fascinating area of collecting. I'm sure that many collectors in Quebec have examples by Richard, Georges Demeules, Edmond Chatigny, Yvon Coté, and other talented carvers in their collections. When these carvings do come on the market via auction or through dealers, prices are substantial.

Jack Craft of Finer Things Antiques & Curios in Halifax was not sure what to expect when he was summoned to the hospital bed of local collector, Reidar David Olsen, who was gravely ill. As it turned out, the collector wanted Craft's help to disperse his superb collection of antique furniture, the majority of which was made in Atlantic Canada. In particular, he was most concerned about an exquisite two-drawer Sheraton stand attributed to 19th-century Halifax cabinet maker, John Tulles (1771–1827). Craft appraised the table at $10,000.

The table is attributed to Tulles based on several distinct features, particularly the inlays, found in his works. In the Sheraton style, it dates to about 1815. The main carcass is constructed of bird's-eye maple with a two-drawer configuration comprising a single drawer over one larger deep drawer faux-fronted to appear as two separate drawers. The cross-banded top is in mahogany. The tapered legs are string-and-dot inlaid terminating in brass caps and casters. Identical inlays have been found on labeled pieces of Tulles furniture and documented in the book, *Heritage Furnishings of Atlantic Canada: A Visual Survey with Pertinent Points* by Henry and Barbara Dobson. The Royal Ontario Museum in Toronto has three pieces of furniture in their collection attributed to Tulles. "It was a collection that was put together over many years and had several excellent 19th-century pieces in it," said Craft. "It was the dying wish of Mr. Olsen who placed his collection with me so that I could find the best possible home for the Tulles table."

It did not take long for Craft to land on the idea of offering the table as a donation to Government House in Halifax. Government House is one of the oldest consecutively occupied government residences, and one of the oldest such official residences in North America.

Two-drawer Sheraton stand, by cabinetmaker John Tulles of Halifax Nova Scotia, early 19th century. Photo courtesy of Government House, Halifax, NS.

He contacted the Executive Director, Christopher McCreery, who immediately expressed interest in the piece and arrangements were made for the table to be donated. "I was pleased to see the table stay here in Halifax and in a setting where everyone can see this terrific example of Tulles' work," said Craft.

Craft recalled how he first crossed paths with Reidar Olsen. "I had known who David was for 20 plus years although he did not know me. I had seen him at local auctions and would always marvel at his discerning eye—he only bought the best of the best. After I opened my store 15 years ago, he became a customer and we struck up a good rapport. It was not too long before we realized we had very similar tastes across many categories, and over the past five years he became one of my most valued customers."

Read more about Reidar Olsen in Appendix Two.

Lachute Flea Market 2014.

Flea Market Finds

Flea markets are an important channel through which antiques and collectibles enter the market. The problem for antique collectors is that a huge amount of other material also shows up at flea markets as well as reproductions. The challenge is to navigate through thousands of items to find the choice antiques and folk art.

Morning at the Lachute Flea Market. 2015.

Every market has its mix of vendors. Some are professionals who set up at more than one market every week, often with much of the same inventory. Others are antique dealers, auctioneers, and collectors looking to sell their items. Many others are individuals who want to downsize their possessions. It is this latter group upon whom the other vendors keep a close eye, for out of their vehicles may emerge something important at a bargain price. If they are unable to go to the flea market, some dealers have

Purchased at the Lachute Flea Market, an excellent wood carving of a horse-drawn sleigh with driver, by John Gagné. Mid 1970s. Author's collection.

scouts—other dealers who buy antiques for them.

It is possible to find underpriced valuable objects in any booth. No individual can know everything in collecting and so good objects can sometimes slip through and be sold at a fraction of their market value. That was the case one day for me at the Lachute flea market in Quebec.

Each Tuesday at the Lachute flea market is antique day. The fields of the market fill with vendors who bring truckloads of items to sell to the thousands of people who come hoping to find a treasure to add to their collections.

Flea markets start early and the Lachute market is no exception. Vendors often set up in the evening or late in the afternoon on Monday to ensure they obtain an optimum location along one of the grassy aisles of the outdoor market. Customers—mostly dealers and keen collectors—begin arriving at first light and roam the market with flashlights to search for the objects they desire. I once arrived late and only a few vendor spaces were available, all of them too small. I asked the owner of the market, who was supervising proceedings from a golf cart, how to determine what constitutes a legitimate "space". He replied simply: "If you can fit your vehicle into it, it's a space."

Purchased at Lachute, a small painted wood carving of a beaver by Wilfrid Richard, late 1970's. Author's collection.

Since receiving the advice from a fellow vendor, I typically arrive at Lachute shortly after dawn and find a convenient spot to park where I can later set up my tables and display the various items I bring to sell. This approach avoids a crowd of helpful individuals cheerfully offering to personally unload your vehicle and, conveniently for them, be first to see what you have brought.

On this particular day, I parked and wandered through the market, looking for folk art pieces to add to my collection. The early morning light was sufficient to see into the vendor's booths. The grass was still wet from an overnight dew and beads of moisture covered the tarps and the objects left exposed to the elements. Small clutches of vendors were gathered here and there, sipping their coffee and chatting quietly. Other individuals wandered the vendor aisles restlessly, doing the same thing as me: searching in hopes of finding a treasure. My radar was tuned to respond to anything that looked interesting, especially folk art.

About thirty feet up one aisle, I casually glanced down at a pile of picture frames stacked vertically and leaning against an old piece of furniture. In the middle of this stack, I noticed the top of a frame with a series of red and yellow circles, looking almost like abstract apples and lemons, painted across the top edge. Those colourful shapes stopped me in my tracks.

Many folk artists are not content to simply paint their subject on a canvas or board; they want to provide as much imagery and information as possible. That often includes painting objects on the frame or on the mat that surrounds the main canvas. It is not unusual to see a frame painted with birds, animals, flowers, or stars.

As collectors know, wishful thinking goes hand in hand with antique or art hunting. Could this frame be holding an interesting work of folk art? Even as I bent down to examine the pile, I was thinking this surely must be a false alarm; just a coincidence that I noticed these quirky, brightly coloured images on a frame buried in a stack of other frames at 6:00 AM at the flea market. I was certain that a quick closer look would verify my doubts.

I held the top edge of the frame immediately in front of the one I was investigating and pulled the first half of the stack forward to look down and see it better. As I peered down and saw the image of a large cat painted on a board within the frame, I knew it was no ordinary cat. This feline image was the work of a well-known Atlantic Canadian folk artist named Joseph Sleep (1914–1978). It was his most iconic subject, known far and wide as a superb folk art image. Looking closer, I could see a large yellow butterfly above the cat. Birds and tulips adorned the left and right side of the painting—more images that Mr. Sleep was known to paint.

I gently tugged on the top of the frame and slowly extracted it from the vertical stack. As the painting slipped up and into full view, there it was! A signature, in pencil across the bottom of the painting, in the artist's hand: *Joseph Sleep*, and the year, *1977*.

The frame had originally held a mirror on a small chest of drawers that Mr. Sleep had repurposed to hold his painting. Not content with that, he painted flowers on the two sides and bottom section of the frame and added bright red and yellow circles across the top, that area being not wide enough for flowers.

Painting of cat with butterfly and flowers in decorated frame, by Joe Sleep, 1977. Author's collection.

Mr. Sleep only painted for a few years toward the end of his life—his was a short but prolific career. His paintings are print-like in that he used the same images, created repeatedly from stencils. Once the stencils were assembled, he would draw in the outlines then paint them.

To say I was surprised at my find that day would be putting it mildly. Mr. Sleep's work is highly collectible and is held in several important galleries, including The Art Gallery of Nova Scotia in Halifax. I rank his work near to that of Maud Lewis (1900–1970) and Joe Norris (1924–1994).

My next task was to try and buy the piece. The vendor was engrossed in a conversation with another dealer and I caught his attention by holding up the painting and waving to him.

"Combien?" I shouted to him. ("How much?" in French).

"Dix!" he replied and quickly turned back to his conversation. For a moment, I thought he meant a thousand dollars! But I realized, no, "dix" is *ten* dollars!

I put the painting down just long enough to get the wallet out of my pocket and extract a ten-dollar bill. I handed him the bill and he did not even turn around, just held out his hand, where I placed the money then turned abruptly on my heel and made a beeline back to my vehicle. I unlocked the door and climbed into the front seat, placing the painting on the passenger side. I pulled out my cell phone and dialed home to tell Joan about this exciting purchase.

In 1981, the Art Gallery of Nova Scotia held a retrospective of Mr. Sleep's work. In the catalogue, guest curator, Bruce Ferguson, writes: "The floating images are stereotypes which act as relatively uncommitted signs. They refer to the real world but not in the usual casual way. Cats do not chase birds, foxes do not chase rabbits and people's lives and their work are eminently stable and useful."

Finding the Joe Sleep painting is a vivid example of why collectors stalk flea markets: to look for the items that somehow slip through the cracks.

Detail of a flower and decorated frame from painting by Joe Sleep. 1977.

Someone else could just as easily have found that painting. But on that day, I was the one who saw the circles painted across the top of the frame and took a moment to peer into the stack to satisfy my curiosity. I have found other nice paintings since then but none under those kinds of circumstances.

As a collector, if you want to get your blood running, start visiting flea markets. And, get there early!

Laurin Garland, Past President of the Canadian Decoy and Outdoor Collectibles Association, being interviewed at the annual show and sale.

8

The Decline of Stories About Antiques in Canadian Media

There is precious little coverage about antiques and collectibles in the Canadian media, a situation that irritates me to no end. One likely reason for this is that there may be no editors or producers who collect antiques. If Canadian material history is to become as important to Canadians as I think it should be, the topic needs more coverage. Given the cost of television production, however, the current dearth of coverage is perhaps not surprising.

Fortunately, there are exceptions. Occasionally, stories appear in Canadian media about a record price for a Canadian artist, like one from the Group of Seven. This is good exposure for the auction houses who build their reputations on achieving higher and higher hammer prices for consignors. These prices are far beyond the reach of most collectors, but good returns raise the profile of Canadian artists and make a positive impression with those who own similar items.

In the past few years, I have had the opportunity to combine my skills as a publicist with my interest in antiques

Screen capture of *The Globe and Mail*'s "Favourite Room" February 14, 2019, with Fred Rizner, President, Canadian Antique Dealers Association (CADA).

and folk art and have proven several times that bringing the right story to the right reporter or editor can generate significant coverage.

The Globe and Mail has a feature called "Favourite Room" that highlights a special room in someone's home. On behalf of CADA, and with the cooperation of the *The Globe and Mail*, I was able to interest journalists in rooms in two Canadian homes. One is an impressive home in Port Hope owned by CADA member, Fred Rizner, who operates Cherry Hill Antiques. The other is a beautiful heritage home near Hamilton owned by CADA member, Richard Rumi, of Richard Rumi Antiques. It was gratifying to see the articles and photographs of these homes and their owners.

John Sewell writes an excellent column, "This Old Thing", which appears in several major Canadian newspapers. In each article, he researches antiques based on photos and descriptions submitted by readers and evaluates their market value.

To its credit, the CBC has aired television productions like the Canadian version of the *Antiques Roadshow*, but it ended several years ago. Since its start in 1979, *Antiques Roadshow*, has remained one of the most popular shows on British television. The Canadian version ran for four seasons and ended in 2009. *Canadian Pickers* aired on the History Channel in Canada for three seasons. While the show had failings that were painfully obvious to seasoned collectors and dealers, it did provide coverage of Canadian antiques. Since these two series went off the air, however, no consistent national coverage of Canadian antiques and art has filled the void. Locally, at my instigation, CBC Radio and CTV television have interviewed me on several occasions about Canadian antiques and folk art. At a national level, however, I suspect staff production supervisors and most independent producers know little if anything about Canadian antiques and art. That brings me back to my earlier point about "gatekeepers". As long as the gatekeepers of our mainstream media outlets know little or nothing about the topic, it follows that no productions will be done.

The lack of media attention has a withering domino effect on antiques. If people do not read about antiques in the print media and online, if there is little or no television coverage, then antiques and antique collecting will fall further from public view. In turn, fewer people will stop at antique stores, shows, museums, and galleries that feature antiques. Declining revenue from admission sales will have a negative financial impact on all aspects of the sector, particularly on smaller museums that already have limited budgets. A lack of political champions of Canadian material history at all levels of government is also worrisome.

At some point, I began to pester Rogers Communications Inc. in Ottawa, where Executive Producer, Gavin Lumsden, oversees the creation of several productions with a local flavour. After several emails and telephone calls, Gavin agreed to meet with me. We talked for well over an hour about antiques and I made the point that there was nothing about Canadian antiques currently on television. During the conversation, Gavin mentioned that he had once had a collection of vinyl record albums that included titles that were special to him, like the original Woodstock concert album. He had left the albums at his family home and they somehow found their way into a garage sale. All those years later, I could tell that the loss of the albums was still fresh in Gavin's mind.

Interviewing Barbara Lukaszewicz as part of the Our Antiques Treasures television series, 2019. Produced by Rogers Television, Ottawa.

As a collector, I could sympathize with Gavin. In the current craze of decluttering and minimalism, antique collections and individual antique pieces are susceptible to the impulses of well-meaning individuals to pare down the contents of their parents', grandparents', and relatives' homes. In doing so, a family heirloom, a piece of art, or a valuable antique can easily be tossed out. The last person you want assessing the contents of a residence is someone whose main objective is to empty the space!

A few weeks after our meeting, Gavin ordered six half-hour episodes of a program about antiques and collectibles on behalf of Rogers TV. He assigned Arthur Levitin to direct and produce the series at the impressive production facilities and studios of Rogers TV in Ottawa.

Fortunately, Arthur had been a comic book collector and we could relate on that level. Working with essentially no budget and a small team of dedicated volunteers, we created the series, titled Our Antique Treasures, which aired on Rogers TV in the fall of 2019. It has been rebroadcast several times since.

I had an ace up my sleeve going into the series in that I knew some of the best collectors in Canada and they lived nearby. They all agreed to be part of the show and brought in items from their collections to feature in their episodes. My friend and fellow collector, Don Hewson, even agreed to do a rehearsal show with examples from his superb collection of Canadian decoys.

My guests brought in the most impressive array of items worth many thousands of dollars, including superb Canadian folk art, fascinating ceramics with a Canadian theme, museum-quality furniture, vintage toys, classic advertising, elegant sterling silver, magnificent textiles, mid-century modern objects, decoys, decorated stoneware, and more. For example, long-time collector and dealer in early Canadian advertising and nostalgia, Ken Aubrey, brought in a terrific collection of items related to beer brewing.

Interviewing Ken Aubrey as part of the Our Antiques Treasures television series. Produced by Rogers Television, Ottawa.

The supervisor of a rural landfill site had been in touch with Ken by phone about antiques acquired from people who wanted to dispose of them at the landfill. He had rescued the items and stored them in sheds on the property. For some time, he and Ken traded phone calls trying to find a mutually convenient time for a meeting. Finally, a date and time was arranged, and Ken drove to the landfill. You can imagine his surprise when the man started bringing out one fantastic antique after another. One of the best items was a large colour print of the Union Brewery facility in Ottawa. An extremely rare find in its original oak frame, the print depicted the factory buildings and its beer brands, including the Brading Brewery. Brading's was owned by the Canadian business tycoon, E. P. Taylor (1901–1989), who would later orchestrate the successful consolidation of more than twenty breweries.

Since most people are not collectors, it follows that they are unaware of the current value of Canadian antiques. I remember preparing for one show—my guest had agreed to bring in two or three pieces of furniture and several small accessories, all museum-quality examples, all in original paint.

Late that afternoon as I was walking past Gavin's office, I leaned into the open doorway and said, "Gavin do you want to see what $10,000 worth of Canadian antiques looks like?" I was exaggerating, although not by much, to make the point that there were some special antiques in the studio.

"Sure!" he said, jumping up from his desk.

"C'mon," I replied. "It's in the studio now."

The set was prepared and collector, Dennis Billard, was seated in a chair. The antique furniture was on a riser in front of him: an impressive Lanark County armchair in original paint and a two-drawer Atlantic Canada side table, also in original paint. The accessories were spread out on another table beside him. Gavin gazed at the beautiful Canadian antiques on display and smiled, took it all in, and then turned back to his office. I think he must have been impressed—at least, I hope he was.

I think the fact that Gavin was a collector, even if in a small way, was important. Once you have collected anything, once you have searched, acquired, and preserved—or lost—a special item, even just one object, you are a collector. The emotional chemistry of acquiring something special and, in Gavin's case, losing it, ripples through your cerebral cortex for years to come.

The only difference between Gavin's experience and other collectors is volume. He had a single album collection, while other collectors have dozens if not hundreds of items in their collections. It is quite common to have collections within a collection.

At the time it aired and still to this day, Our Antique Treasures was likely the only television show in Canada devoted exclusively to the topic of antiques and collectibles. I enjoyed making the series and hope to be involved with more productions in the future.

Collectors can be odd people at times: covetous of our collections, competitive when chasing new objects, secretive, and often eccentric, but we have one thing in common: we are immensely proud of our collections and most often willing to share and show the items if the circumstances are right.

Perhaps that is because we share an unsettling feeling that there are not that many people coming behind us who have discovered the joy of collecting. Where is the next generation of Canadian collectors? Who will step up to be the next custodians of all the cultural material that sits outside of our regional and national museums and galleries?

> *"Where is the next generation of Canadian collectors? Who will step up to be the next custodians of all the cultural material that sits outside of our regional and national museums and galleries?"*

Genuine Canadian antiques have been lost in a veritable sea of often questionable material. The age of many new objects is no longer a distinguishing factor; sometimes, they are virtually new things dressed up to look old. Often, if an object simply looks old, has a popular colour, is priced correctly, and serves a purpose, it is "collectible"—meaning, really, that it will sell. Interior design magazines abound with photos of used furniture tarted up with the latest popular paint colours. A new coat of paint on a piece of furniture does not impart integrity. If the underlying object is a two-dollar chair, then the same chair with a stylish new coat of paint is still worth two dollars.

The one certainty I had going into Our Antique Treasures was that the twelve collectors taking part in the series had high standards in terms of what they collected and what they were bringing into the studio to discuss. All the antiques and folk art were of superb quality. They would score high marks on any collector's checklist. Visually, that is what made the series a success.

More media coverage of our cultural history could cause more Canadians to start collecting. I was a young collector once; I am no longer. I find myself in the same predicament as other older collectors, with no one in my family who will take over my collection. It will likely go to auction where market forces will dictate the financial return and next destinations of the prized objects with which we have lived for so many years.

On a more positive note, the pandemic has forced us all, including our cultural institutions, to improve our use of digital applications. A greater abundance of online content about Canada's material history may cause, over time, an increase in the number of collectors. We will just have to wait to find out. Who knows, it might even cause the creation of a new television series.

Small oil on canvas of men fishing from a birchbark canoe. Painting dates to the 1920's. Author's collection.

9
Gone Fishin'

Like so many other collectors, Joan and I have collections within our collection of country furniture and folk art. One such sub-set comprises my fishing-related collectibles.

As a young boy and well into my teenage years, I spent just about every summer at the family cottage in Quebec. The lake was the anchor of our outdoor activities, of which fishing figured prominently in the mix—along with berry picking, hiking, and intense badminton games in the parking lot behind the cottage.

I began to collect fishing-related memorabilia in part because Joan and I bought our own cottage in 1998. The property came with the original cottage, a sleep cabin, out buildings, and all the contents. The old boat house contained a vintage, fourteen-foot, cedar-strip Peterborough runabout and a canvas/cedar-strip canoe built by the Dey Brothers, who had been in business around 1890 to 1910. Their name was on a faded label on the bow of the canoe, along with their address: Laurier Bridge, Ottawa.

Cleaning out the buildings, some of which dated to the early 1900s, was a chore, but we knew there might be the odd treasure tucked away in a trunk or blanket box. We had help from my brothers (Scott, Sloan, and Stuart), all avid fishermen, and it was

Old wooden rowboat oars are sought after by collectors.

Sloan who discovered a cache of fishing lures tucked into a large tin in one of the sheds. I remember he burst out the door of the shed, shouting: "Look, what I found!" Inside the tin were twenty or thirty lures, some of them dating to about 1910. For his help on that occasion and others, I happily gifted him with the lure collection. We continued to find interesting fishing rods and reels that Scott and Stuart gladly accepted as gifts.

A pair of paint decorated miniature canoe paddles from Quebec, 1942. Author's collection.

Accessories like old paddles, "crooked" knives (used in canoe construction) and canoe cups (carried by paddlers to dip into the water) are also popular with collectors, especially items carved and decorated with animal forms or geometric designs.

Years before buying our cottage, I received a call from a woman living near us in the west end of Ottawa. She had antiques to sell, and I agreed to visit. One of the things I bought from her that day was a superb canoe paddle that featured a landscape painting on the blade. The scene depicted a camp on a river with a canoe pulled up on the shore and a white tent set up at the edge of the forest. She said the image was of a camp on an island in the Ottawa River. I believe the paddle and the painting date to about

1900. I have bought many paddles since, but this one remains the best in my collection.

Paddle with island camping scene painted on the blade, Ottawa River, c. 1900. Author's collection.

Another favourite paddle I found hanging on a wall in a small, local antique shop. It is a crudely made wooden canoe paddle that obviously served someone well over the years. The owner thought enough of it to paint the words "Ottawa River" on the blade with what I presume to be a date, "49", at the base of the handle. I suspect the paddle was made for use in a canvas/cedar strip canoe, which at the time would have been common along the Ottawa River.

I am also fond of a decorated paddle I found in an antique shop in Prince Edward County. I wandered through the shop without seeing anything of interest until I noticed the paddle tucked high up on a cross-beam. I could tell it had age, but what really piqued my interest was the painted decoration on the blade.

The owner of the shop somewhat reluctantly brought the paddle down for my inspection. Once I had it in my hands, I could tell it dated to at least the 1940s and likely earlier. The decoration painted on it was the amusing image of Donald Duck with the word "Babs" written in balloon-type letters beneath. The paddle was in good original condition and I was interested in buying it.

Rather emphatically, the shop owner said, "The paddle is for sale and the price is $100."

Crudely made paddle signed '49 Ottawa River. Author's collection.

I was taken aback, as I had never paid that kind of money for a paddle. I tried to negotiate and failed. "The price," he repeated just as emphatically a second time, "is $100."

I could tell by the way he spoke that I was far from the first person to express an interest in this paddle. Who knows how many others had inquired about it then walked away when they heard the price? I turned away, too, and he put it back in its spot on the cross-beam while likely dismissing me as yet another collector unwilling to meet his price.

I took a few steps down the aisle of the store and stopped, turned back to him and said, "I'll take the paddle."

Imagine the stories these paddles could tell! Like most antiques, though, they will keep their secrets about their makers and their many adventurous trips on the lakes and rivers of Eastern Ontario and Western Quebec.

Birchbark Canoes and Canoe Cups

Along with paddles, a dealer or picker may occasionally come across a vintage birch-bark canoe in a barn or outbuilding in the Ottawa Valley. It is always an exciting find, as early birch-bark canoes can be worth thousands of dollars depending on their condition.

I once discovered a child-size bark canoe, about six feet long, nestled in the rafters of an old frame cottage just west of Ottawa. As is often the case, though, finding an antique is one thing and buying it is another! Try as I might, I could not convince the owners to sell me the canoe and, as far as I know, the little beauty is still resting up there.

The Babs paddle, decorated about 1930. Author's collection.

They did, however, sell me an excellent canoe cup with the image of a dancing couple scratch-carved on the underside. The cup handle was further embellished with a scratch-carved moose head. I believe the cup dated to about 1900 and I proudly displayed it on a wall in a stairwell at home. One day, the late Jason Miskelly noticed the cup while visiting. He asked for a price and I quoted what I thought was a higher-than-reasonable amount, $250. Without hesitation, Jason bought the cup. It is difficult to know what the top-end price for a quality antique may be. Jason had no difficulty selling it sometime later, and I presume the price at that point would have been $350 or more.

Fishing-Themed Folk Art

I have also collected a number of folk art paintings related to fishing. Several depict fishermen in the midst of catching or casting for fish. The earliest in my collection are a pair of small oil-on-canvas scenes. Unframed, unsigned, and quite fragile, I found them sitting on a table at a flea market.

Folk art painting of fishermen at their camp, oil on board. Mid 1940s. Author's collection.

The style of a painting and details like the clothes people are wearing can often help date a piece. The reverse side can also hold clues. Canvas changes colour with time as do the wooden frames which hold the painting. The effect is called "air burn", a progressive darkening of the original wood or canvas. The atmosphere in which a painting hangs can contribute to discolouration. Sooty air from an open fireplace, pipe or cigarette smoke causes air burn. Based on the air burn of these paintings and other clues, I suspected they were created in the early 1920s.

Painting by Cliff Grier signed by the artist and dated 1942. Author's collection.

Another flea-market find in my collection is a painting depicting a lake scene with a log cabin and a man standing outside the front door. He gazes excitedly down to the lake, where his buddy has just pulled a bark canoe up

Painted iron figure of a fisherman catching a fish. Possibly a sign for a cabin or lodge. Mid 1950's. Author's collection.

onto the shoreline. The man standing beside the canoe holds up a string of large fresh-caught fish. Interestingly, he faces the viewer and not his friend, although the artist's choice makes perfect sense because, facing the other way, his back would conceal the fresh fish from us.

At an estate sale many years ago, I was pleased to acquire a large oil-on-board painting by Clifton (Cliff) Wellington Greer (1904 – 1986). The painting is titled, "Strike! Severn River, Muskoka". Dated 1942, it features two fishermen in a birch-bark canoe and a fish that appears to have taken the bait in that very moment. It is a terrific painting and, while not an example of folk art, it fits nicely into my collection-within-a-collection of fishing-related antiques and collectibles.

Oil on canvas of man fishing in a lake. Unsigned. Likely Quebec, 1950's. Author's collection.

My most unusual piece of folk art related to fishing was acquired at the Gatineau Historical Society's annual antique auction a few years ago. It is a painted sign that says: "Worms for Sale/Vers a Vendre". There were giggles and snorts of laughter when the piece came up for sale, but I was not laughing—I thought the sign was terrific.

The artist was not content with simply painting words on the sign; they also embellished it with almost impressionistic flowers in bright colours against a black background. The sign reminds me of one Maud Lewis created in the 1960s to advertise her paintings for sale. It, too, was painted on a black background; Lewis' featured birds and flowers in addition to the lettering. At the auction that day, I was the only person to raise my hand

Painted sign oil on masonite board, created about 1950. Author's collection.

and brought the sign home for the princely sum of $5. I had it framed and it continues to bring me great satisfaction.

Fishing collectibles continue to be popular, perhaps because of the sense of connection they embody. It is quite a feeling to step into a canvas-covered, cedar-strip canoe, push off from the shore of a pristine Quebec lake, and quietly dip a seventy-five-year-old paddle into the water to propel you down the same waterways upon which indigenous peoples and pioneers relied for centuries. Each piece of fishing-themed folk art gives me a similar feeling. Not many things in life are this subtly gratifying.

Blake and Ruth McKendry's vehicle loaded with antiques, early 1960s.

10

EARLY OTTAWA ANTIQUE DEALERS, BLAKE AND RUTH MCKENDRY

In 1955, Blake McKendry and his wife, Ruth, opened The Pioneer Shop on Elgin Street in Ottawa, specializing in the sale of early Canadian antiques and rare books. It strikes me now that the name of their store had a double meaning. They were buying, collecting, and selling antiques from the "pioneer" period of Canadian history; and, opening a store of that nature in 1958 made them pioneers in the Canadian antiques trade.

In his Foreword to Blake McKendry's book, the Canadian art historian, Russell Harper (1914 – 1983), wrote that "less than twenty five years ago the first exhibition of Canadian folk painting was hung in the National Gallery, Ottawa. It was greeted with a mixture of disapproval, questioning and cynicism. Since that time a warm acceptance of these simple forms has developed that demonstrates a maturing and intense delight in Canada's folk expressions."

By comparison, folk art collecting in the U.S. began thirty years earlier, around 1920, when a few individuals recognized the importance of American-made folk art and country antiques. At that point, American folk art was

The McKendry's Pioneer Shop on Elgin Street in Ottawa, 1958.

largely dismissed as unimportant and well beneath the popular antiques and art of the times.

When Electra Havermeyer Webb (1888 – 1960) started to collect American country antiques and folk art, her mother called it "American trash". Mrs. Webb and her husband, James Watson Webb, (1884 – 1960) would go on to build a collection of American folk art that ultimately became the Shelburne Museum at their farm in Shelburne, Vermont.

Juliana Reiser Force (1876 – 1948), the first Director of the Whitney Gallery of American Art, returned to her ancestral roots in 1914 when she and her husband, Willard Force (? – 1928), bought a farm in Bucks County, Pennsylvania. She decorated her new home with antiques and folk art, much of it based on Pennsylvania Germanic influences. The first curated shows of folk art in the United States, including one organized by Mrs. Force, were held in the early 1920s.

In 1925, Nina Fletcher Little (1903 – 1993) and her husband bought an unrestored log home near Boston as a getaway. On the advice of a cousin, an ardent collector of American antiques and folk art, the couple began to buy affordable New England area country antiques. They soon discovered folk art and Mrs. Little began collecting and conducting important research in the field, especially documenting the work of itinerant portrait painters.

The Abby Aldrich Rockefeller Folk Art Collection opened at Colonial Williamsburg in Williamsburg, Virginia in 1935. By that time, Abby Rockefeller (1878 – 1948) had been collecting folk art for years, buying pieces for her collection from Edith Halpert, who was among the first dealers to display folk art in her American Folk Art Gallery in New York City.

Perhaps the McKendrys were influenced by these trends and individuals south of the border. Their daughter, Jennifer McKendry, recalled, in an interview with me, that her father deeply admired a book by Wallace Nutting about American furniture.

I also interviewed long-time antique dealer, publisher, show convenor, and collector, Bill Dobson, who summarized the early years of antiquing in Canada and his interactions with the McKendrys:

> "I got to know them at an early antique show in Kingston, Ontario, at an Anglican Church. It was a show that went on for a long time and the McKendrys were always there. I remember sitting down and talking to Blake. He was a quiet person but quite deep.

He was the one that encouraged young people to start collecting.

"He talked to me about Canadiana and about trying to acquire pieces that were not manufactured. He also taught me the true value of folk art and the differences between good utilitarian folk art pieces and those that had an artistic flair to them. Blake was the one who really got me to start distinguishing the differences between pieces, not so much with furniture but with folk art. He explained the differences between good, better, and best."

Bill points to Expo '67 as the event that caused Canadians nation-wide to start thinking about the material history of Canada, prompted the creation of many local museums, caused many people to start collecting, and inspired some to write books on the subject. The McKendrys were at the forefront of this trend.

Mrs. McKendry was a passionate collector of Canadian quilts and bed coverings. In 1979, three years of intense and focused work culminated in the publication of her book, *Quilts and Other Bed Coverings in the Canadian Tradition*.

In the *Ottawa Journal* on December 29, 1979, reviewer Stevie Cameron described the book as a "major contribution to the history of Canadian folk art and the comprehensive study of Canadian quilts, coverlets, bedding and bed furniture." The 450 photographs in the book (118 of them in colour) were all taken by Mr. McKendry. Mrs. McKendry also wrote a second book, *Classic Quilts*, again featuring photographs taken by her husband.

Mrs. McKendry's personal collection of quilts and coverlets eventually reached 315 in number. In 1979, she sold the collection to what is now called the Canadian

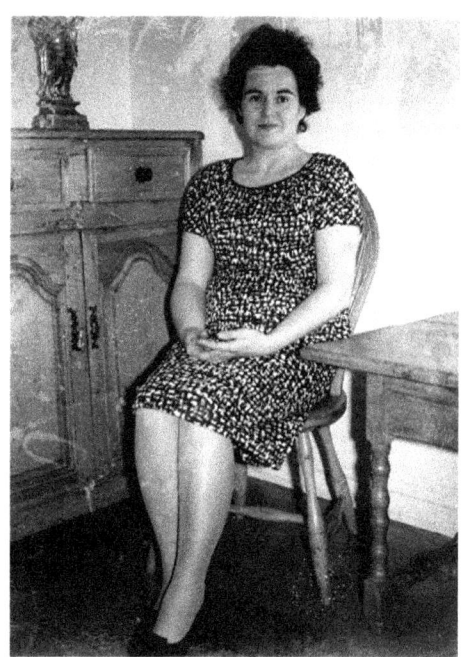

Ruth McKendry about 1958.

Museum of History. In 2002, the museum acquired a second collection of textiles from her.

Bill Dobson credits Mrs. McKendry for his interest in textiles. As a result of his conversations with her, he and his wife, Linda Hynes, assembled a superb collection of textiles. "It was Ruth who got me interested in homespun blankets and woven coverlets. At the early antique shows in the 1970s, I would talk with Ruth and Dorothy Burnham (1911 – 2004), who wrote the book on textiles: *Keep Me Warm One Night*. I would confer with those two ladies at all the early antique shows."

Blake McKendry about 1958.

In 2017, at the Warden's Banquet (Bill was Warden of Lanark County that year), he and Linda donated their entire collection of textiles—eighty homespun blankets and overshot coverlets—to the Textile Museum in Almonte, Ontario.

A McKendry vehicle after an antique buying trip. Early 1960s.

As Jennifer McKendry pointed out to me in an email exchange, her parents successfully ran their shop on Elgin Street until 1961. Her mother oversaw the day-to-day operations, while her father worked as a patent attorney in a law firm a few blocks north of the store in downtown Ottawa.

The McKendrys would spend their weekends hunting for antiques, most frequently in the province of Quebec, and often accompanied by the late Dr. Herbert T. Schwarz and famed collector, Nettie Covey Sharpe (1907 – 2002). As Mr. McKendry notes in his introduction to *Folk Art*, "During this early period we were primarily concerned with naïve early Quebec religious sculpture, naïve paintings and secular sculpture of a past generation, weathervanes, including weather cocks, hooked rugs and some painted furniture."

The McKendrys also had the benefit of regular visits from staff members

Every space in the McKendry vehicle filled with antiques. Early 1960s.

of the National Gallery of Canada in Ottawa, who would frequently stop by the store to discuss recently acquired pieces.

According to their daughter, a significant change occurred when dealers started buying and selling Ontario antiques. Quebec antiques were thought to be earlier than Ontario items—18th century versus 19th century—so dealers tended to focus on buying the older material from Quebec. Over time, however, dealers began to embrace Ontario antiques. "My parents were among the earlier collectors to acquire Ontario furniture probably in the late 1950s and for sure by 1960."

> *"My parents were among the earlier collectors to acquire Ontario furniture probably in the late 1950s and for sure by 1960."*
>
> — Jennifer McKendry

In 1961, the McKendrys moved to Perth, Ontario, about fifty miles west of Ottawa. When their daughter finished high school and left home for university, they acted on a desire for a large country property and purchased one hundred acres near Sharbot Lake, forty miles west of Perth. There, they built a house, and later a barn, for selling antiques.

In 1970, the McKendrys made another move, this time to 2935 Latimer Road just north of Kingston, Ontario, into a limestone house originally built in 1820 by Tunis Snook (1785–1878). Their plan was to restore the house, as much as possible, to its original condition. The house had been neglected but much of the interior remained intact, including original woodwork.

Drawing on their expertise, the McKendrys slowly restored the home in keeping with the period and decorated it with their personal collection of furniture, textiles, folk

McKendry advertisement for the shop in Perth, Ontario.

art, lighting, and accessories. They also kept antiques in the existing barn, but soon built a separate building in which Mrs. McKendry had her own space for textiles.

They must have known that the Snook house was to be their "jewel in the crown", the ultimate piece in their collection. It was a restoration project of significant proportions and detail, and one of the most interesting and historic stone homes in Eastern Ontario.

In February 1980, the restored Snook house was featured in the magazine, *Canadian Antiques & Art Review*. The author, James T. Wills, writes: "To stand between the hearth and the panelled wall opposite is to return to the calm beauty of Loyalist Upper Canada." Yet, while the house was historically important and a showcase for their collections, the McKendrys saw the 200-year-old Georgian structure as their residence. They are quoted in the article as saying: "The Tunis Snook Farm is not a 'restoration' as such, nor is it a museum, it is what it has always been … a home."

The Tunis Snook Farm near Kingston, Ontario.

Mr. McKendry was a publishing dynamo. Early on, he turned his attention to Canadian folk art and the books he wrote and published formed the foundation of knowledge on Canadian folk artists both traditional and contemporary. He authored *Folk Art: Primitive and Naïve Art in Canada* (1983), the introduction of which is one of the most informative and insightful essays on Canadian folk art that I have ever read. He followed it with *A Dictionary of Folk Artists in Canada from the 17th Century to the Present* (1988), *A to Z of Canadian Art, Artists & Art Terms* (1997), *An Illustrated Companion to Canadian Folk Art* (1999), *The New A to Z of Canadian Art* (2001), and *Key Dates in Canadian Art* (with Jennifer McKendry, 2001).

In addition to writing, Mr. McKendry also assisted museums and art galleries in their acquisition of historic Canadian paintings and sculptures and he was a recognized appraiser and consultant on Canadian art and antiques.

Two customers load their truck at the McKendry farm / antique store in 1974.

In 1992, the McKendrys made their final move, to 9 Baiden Street in Kingston, Ontario, where they retired as dealers and moved next door to their daughter, continuing to write articles and books. Prior to the move, they held an on-site auction of their collections, including the furnishings and folk art from their stone farmhouse, on the weekend of August 20, 1993. Joan and I attended the sale, which made for an exciting and memorable day. Collections like the McKendrys' rarely come to auction, but when they do, collectors arrive in droves and push prices for the rarest or best-quality items to new heights. The McKendry sale was no exception.

Blake McKendry carrying a table during set up at a Kingston antique show. Late 1970s.

The Mckendry auction conducted by Tim Potter Auction Services under a tent at the Tunis Snook farm.

Carol Telfer of Carol Telfer Antiques, herself an expert on Canadian textiles including quilts, hooked mats, and samplers, wrote to me with her thoughts on Mrs. McKendry: "Although I did not personally interact with Ruth McKendry, she was a mentor through her books, love of textiles and the articles that I would enthusiastically read in order to learn as much as I could regarding textiles in Canada. Ruth McKendry was definitely the Canadian icon for textiles and their history."

Carol followed up with a story about another interesting hooked rug in the McKendry sale: "This sweet rug was in the McKendry home in 1974. The rug was sold at the McKendry sale back in the late '80s and it went into a renowned collection and remained there until a year ago when I purchased it and did some conservation work to put it back into shape as well as a serious cleaning and then it was sewn onto a stretcher. I love the rug—such a feeling of warmth and love along with the abstract and primitive workmanship expressing the creativity of the maker who hooked the mat. I can certainly appreciate why the McKendrys also loved this mat and included it in their book. It is now hanging in my home in Gagetown, New Brunswick. Lucky me!"

Jennifer McKendry recalls that the National Gallery of Canada acquired carvings and furniture from her parents and from Dr. Herbert Schwartz in the 1950s and 1960s. Jennifer also noted the opening of Upper Canada Village in 1961 as a seminal event in the appreciation of Canadian antiques.

Among the various items she sent me about the McKendrys was this eloquent and touching tribute to them written by their friend and colleague, Philip Shackleton. Auctioneer, Tim Potter, read it aloud at the final auction of the McKendrys' remaining collection on November 22, 2003:

"Blake and Ruth McKendry have lived through a period in which Canadians' attitude to their own heritage has changed immensely. To look back fifty years and more, to recall the lack of concern for the fate of the material memorabilia left to us by predecessors is to conjure a period that seems indeed strange. Our awakening to the values associated with the legacy of past generations is indeed very recent. And that awakening to such a large extent has been due to the pioneering spirit and dedicated work of collectors and dealers like Ruth and Blake.

"As very active people, whose knowing hands have touched so many pieces of what we now call our own fine art or fine crafts, they have been pace setters in nurturing the appreciation for our own domestic treasures. And the books that they have written and published have become our standards of reference.

"As collectors they have lived with some of the finest and most fascinating material from their Canadian background. And they have shared with fellow collectors the opportunity to enjoy, to become familiar with, and also to live with, some of the most meaningful of those treasures.

"One special thing about Blake: He didn't totally deny the value of public galleries and museums as custodians of reference collections. But he had a very special regard for the private collector. He respected and encouraged the role of the private enthusiast in seeking out, in preserving and establishing meaningful worth for products of the human past.

"He reminded us too that a treasure in a museum is a treasure out of reach. While a treasure held by a private collector is very likely to come back again someday to the marketplace. So that new collectors will enjoy the opportunity to acquire something of the best.

"We salute a personal legacy of great value. We treasure wonderful memories of shared memories and shared enthusiasm. And we are most grateful that Blake and Ruth are sharing the fruit of their collecting years with the collectors of this day and the collectors of tomorrow."

Blake McKendry passed away in 2003 and Ruth McKendry followed three years later. One can only be deeply impressed by the dedication this couple exhibited and by their passion for Canadian material history. They focused their collecting and research on categories at the heart of Canadian antiques: textiles, furniture, accessories, and folk art both traditional and contemporary. Their deep involvement enriched a nascent field during a period when Canada was slowly beginning to appreciate its material history.

The McKendrys' legacy lives on in the books they wrote, photographed, and published; in the collections they donated; and, in the collections they advised others to assemble—rich resources that will educate new collectors for years to come.

Charles Vollrath wood carver. Mid 1940's. Photo from an article by the late Brenda Lee Whiting.

Beauty in Wood: Folk Art Masters of the Ottawa Valley

A sub-genre of folk art collecting in Canada, woodcarving is exceptionally popular. Wood was always in abundance in Canada and a pocketknife was the only tool needed to transform a block of it into a piece of art. The Ottawa Valley was home to several folk artists who worked in wood. Here, I'll focus on three whom I know from experience and whose work I either collect or helped other people to collect.

Charles Vollrath (Chalk River, Ontario)

Charles Vollrath (1870 – 1952) was immensely talented and his carvings of wildlife, angels and other religious items are highly sought after by collectors. Mr. Vollrath was active in the 1930s and '40s, producing wood carvings that he sold to tourists at a roadside stand. From that small stand, his carvings were distributed throughout Canada, the U.S., and beyond.

Charles Vollrath's great grandson, Chad Vollrath, read my first book, *Folk Art in the Attic,* which included a passage about his great-grandfather. Chad wanted to find a carving by the elder Vollrath to give as a gift to his father and emailed me for help. I knew his search would be challenging. I certainly did not have a Vollrath carving in my collection and it had been several years since I had seen one. I told him I would keep an eye open. My luck would come a few months later when I decided to make the rounds of a few antique stores in downtown Ottawa, including one that I visited only infrequently.

I climbed the stairs to the second level of a building on Bank Street that housed the antique store, said hello to the owner/dealer, and proceeded to wander through the maze of rooms piled high with all manner of books, paintings, antiques, and various collectables. Some antique dealers prefer the "jumble" approach: pile stuff everywhere and anywhere in the shop and let customers have the fun and the challenge of searching for a particular item. This dealer took that model to a whole new level.

I wandered here and there and returned to where he was seated in a chair near the entrance. We chatted for a few moments about the state of the antique business in general. It was about 2:00 PM as I stood next to a table brimming with small antiques. My left foot was touching a stack of paintings piled on the floor. I could hear traffic on the busy street outside and weak sunlight struggled through the dusty windows.

An elderly man emerged from the entrance hallway and took a few steps into the shop area, where he paused in front of us. His breathing was laboured from coming up the long flight of stairs up to the shop. He wore a beige overcoat a few sizes too large. In his left hand, he carried a large paper shopping bag and jutting out from the top of it were the wooden antlers of a moose carving. My eyes immediately locked on to the bag and I blurted: "Hey, is that a Vollrath or Patterson carving?" (Abe Patterson (1899 – 1969) was another talented carver from the Ottawa Valley whose work is also highly sought after.)

"Why, yes, it is by Vollrath," the man replied, somewhat startled by my question.

He sat down heavily in the armchair across from the dealer, placing the bag on the floor in front of him. Slowly, he reached down, extracted the piece from the bag and held it up

Five foot tall moose carved by Charles Vollrath, likely early to mid 1940s. Image courtesy of John Wright who took the original photograph.

for inspection by the dealer. I knew immediately this was an impressive carving by Charles Vollrath and, of course, I was anxious to buy it. The dealer reached over, took the carving and began to examine it. The old man explained that he had broken one of the antlers getting it out of the car. Fortunately, he had the broken piece with him, and I knew it would be a relatively easy repair.

I asked to take a closer look at the piece and quickly saw that Mr. Vollrath had also carved his surname in large upper-case letters into the base at the feet of the moose. I also found a paper label tacked to the underside of the carving. In faint hand-written black letters were the words: "*Made by Charles Vollrath, Chalk River, Ontario*".

Chad Vollrath with his great grandfather's carving of a moose.

"Are you going to sell that?" I asked the old man.

"Are you interested in it?"

"Yes, I am."

"Well, make me an offer."

I paused because it would be a serious breach of etiquette to attempt a direct transaction with the man, thereby removing the dealer from the

Small promotional handout for Charles Vollrath. Early 1930's.

process. I changed tactics and turned to the dealer, asking, "Are you going to buy it?"

"I might," he replied.

"Well, if you do, I'm interested."

They continued to chat while I stood by, then I wandered off several paces to give them time to make their transaction. I realized it might take longer than I thought, retraced my steps, and said, "I tell you what. Why don't I leave you to it? I'm going to go for a walk."

The dealer turned to me, reached for a pen and piece of paper, and said, "Well, give me your number so I can call you."

"Why don't I come back in an hour?" I replied.

"That's fine," the dealer said. "Come back then."

I left the shop and continued my rounds of other antique stores then made a trip to the bank to pick up some funds to complete the transaction, should I be fortunate enough to acquire the carving.

An hour later, I walked back into the store, where the dealer was still sitting by the front entrance. The old man was gone and there was no sign of the carving.

We chatted for a few minutes and he confirmed, much to my relief, that the carving was now in his possession. I then told him I knew the carver's great-grandson and wanted to buy the piece so I could sell it to him and fulfill the dream he had of acquiring one of these carvings to give to his father.

The name C. Vollrat is carved into the base.

Cardboard note tacked to bottom of a Vollrath carving. It reads: "Made by Charles Vollrath, Chalk River, Ontario."

We quickly agreed on a modest price and he retrieved it from a room where he had it in safekeeping.

I drove home thinking about the fortunate set of circumstances that had occurred. At home, I took a photograph of the carving then sent an email message to Chad. He replied a few minutes later and I gave him an account of what had just transpired. He was excited to see the photo of the carving now in my possession.

Completing the transaction was one of those magical moments that occur in collecting. This majestic carving created by Charles Vollrath some eighty-five years ago was going back to the Vollrath family.

Since that memorable day, I have found more carvings by Charles Vollrath that Chad has added to his collection. Well known dealer, Larry Foster, later discovered a small promotional flyer that Mr. Vollrath must have made in the 1940s. I bought it for Chad, too, as he had not seen one.

Chad's great-grandfather often carved large examples of wildlife. A few years ago, I was made aware of a large Vollrath carving of a deer coming up for auction in a small town south of Ottawa. I arranged to see the piece beforehand and sent an email to Chad describing it. This could potentially be another important acquisition for the family. Chad drove from Sarnia, Ontario with his father to be at the sale. I stood beside them to watch. The Vollrath carving came up and after some modest bidding was knocked down to Chad. As I recall, the price was around $350.

Chad Vollrath and his father, Glenn Vollrath, stand with their auction purchase, the large deer by Charles Vollrath.

Chad and his father were elated, and I was happy for them. As we chatted, Pierre Menard, a good friend of mine and a keen folk art collector, approached us. In confidence, he said: "I would have kept on bidding on the deer, but I heard that the family wanted to buy this carving. So, I stopped bidding." There may be no friends at an auction, but on that day, Pierre Menard was a good friend to the Vollrath family.

Charles Vollrath was a true folk artist. While on occasion he and Abe Patterson met to discuss carving techniques, he was likely self-taught. Like many folk artists, he successfully sold his carvings and repeated successful examples. Yet his carving of a small angel probably says more about his exceptional talent than any other piece he created. It is executed with a simple charm and, like excellent folk art, also makes a powerful religious and spiritual statement. This little carving says as much about the considerable folk art talent of Charles Vollrath than perhaps anything else he created.

Abe Patterson (Pembroke, Ontario)

Perhaps the most famous of the upper Ottawa Valley wood carvers, Abe Patterson (1899 – 1969) had a long and productive career of several decades. He, too, carved wildlife subjects, including full-size bears, horse-drawn logging sleighs and wagons, hunters in canoes, totem poles, as well as home decor items, sports trophies, and even hockey players.

Mr. Patterson spent a good part of his childhood roaming the woods near his home in Greenwood off old Highway 17, a few miles from Pembroke. Wood carving was a pastime for much of his early life, and at thirty-five years old, he made the momentous decision to quit his position at a Pembroke factory to take up wood carving full time. The year before, Canada had weathered its worst economic depression and the unemployment rate had reached thirty percent. Leaving a full-time position just a year later would have been a serious decision for anyone, but in Mr. Patterson's case, it proved to be the right one.

Like Charles Vollrath, Mr. Patterson had to find a market for his work, so he modified an old vehicle and offered his carvings for sale at the side of Highway 17. One of his customers was associated with sportsmen's shows in the U.S. Feeling that the talented woodcarver would be a colourful and interesting addition to the show's attractions, he offered Mr. Patterson a contract. Patterson accepted and the move would transform him into one of the best-known wood carvers in North America. For several years thereafter, he appeared at shows throughout Canada and the U.S., selling his work and carving on site as well.

In 2014, I had the opportunity to interview Abe Patterson's son, the late Alexander "Pat" Patterson (1938 – 2017). He welcomed me into his home and we talked about his father's career as a woodcarver. Pat was rightfully proud of his father's accomplishments, particularly the challenging projects, like the large totem poles he carved entirely by himself.

Pat recalled an occasion in 1961 when his father was asked if he could carve something as an entrance feature to the Department of Lands and Forest logging exhibit in Algonquin Park, Ontario. Mr. Patterson happily accepted the challenge and carved a life-size figure of a lumberjack holding an axe. Departmental management must have been pleased, because the lumberjack would grace the entrance for fifty years. The carving finally succumbed to the elements and the institute decided to replace it.

"I found out about it and called them," Pat said. "I asked them what they were going to do with the one my father carved."

"And what did they tell you?" I asked.

"Throw it out! That's what they told me." Pat said he responded quickly: "Don't do that! I'll take it."

Although the lumberjack carving was weather-beaten and layered in numerous coats of preservative stain, Pat wasted no time driving to the institute, loading up the carving, and bringing it home. The sign was replaced by an exact copy cast in bronze.

In 1958, the City of Pembroke commissioned a large totem pole to adorn public property there. Mr. Patterson happily took on the project and carved and painted a forty-five-foot totem that now resides at the Pembroke Museum. In the early 1960s, he accepted an assignment to carve a thirty-six-foot-high totem pole for Garfield Weston's lodge near Mattawa, followed by several others that supported the building's wrap-around porch.

Abe Patterson was a prolific carver, yet his work is not easily found today. When pieces do turn up, collectors snap them up for prices upwards of $3,000 and more for large examples.

Gavin Wilson, an antique dealer and picker, has handled several Patterson carvings over the years. One of his favourite pieces is called Home-

Abe Patterson carving at a show, about 1950.

ward Bound, which he purchased for $800 from a dealer at an outdoor antique show years ago. The dealer had bought the carving on a house-call in a small town in the Ottawa Valley. Another dealer to whom Gavin had previously sold many antiques saw the carving and immediately wanted to buy it. Gavin declined, stating that his plans were to keep the carving in his personal collection. The dealer then referred to their previous transactions. This is a common strategy in the collecting field and it is difficult to decline the request of a good customer who has consistently bought pieces from you over time. The loyalty play was effective and, somewhat reluctantly, Gavin sold the carving for $3,200—quite likely a top price for a Patterson work at the time.

Several months later, Gavin happened to visit the dealer's home and found him loading his vehicle for an antique show. Much to his surprise, the big Patterson carving was in the load destined for the show! This time, it was Gavin's turn to put on the pressure. If that carving was going to be sold again, he wanted to be the buyer. The dealer agreed to sell the carving back to Gavin but not at a loss. Gavin paid the $3,200 asking price and the big carving returned home with him.

Homeward Bound wood carving by Abe Patterson. Private collection.

Remarkably, Abe Patterson carved Homeward Bound out of one solid piece of pine. This masterpiece is two feet in length and six inches in height. It features a hunter paddling home with a large deer, a buck, stored in the centre portion of a canoe; the hunter's pack is stored behind the tall bow. The piece likely dates to the late 1950s or early 1960s.

Merely by putting well-placed notches in the wood, Mr. Patterson was able to simulate the look of the seams of birch bark as well as the gunnels wrapped in de-barked spruce root. The base is carved to look like waves pushing up against the canoe. Judging from the hat and the securely fastened coat worn by the hunter, it is late autumn as he pushes for home against a brisk wind, paddle resting in the water at the end of a stroke.

According to Gavin, Mr. Patterson did not like to paint his carvings, preferring to either leave them in the natural colour of the wood or to simply stain them. However, he would paint a piece if a customer asked him to do so. And what a painter he was! I saw a magnificent painted Patterson carving of a log driver with a team of four horses. I did not buy it because, although the price was originally $700, by the time I arrived in Petawawa to see it the owner had raised the price to $1,000. I should have bought it anyway.

The Harness Racer carving by Abe Patterson. Mid 1950's. Private collection.

Abe Patterson became something of a legend in Pembroke. Building on his popularity, the local tourist authority published a promotional pamphlet about him. Titled *The Story of Abe Patterson, World Famous Wood Carving Marvel of Pembroke, Ontario*, the text includes this paragraph:

The Fish and Chips wagon wood carving by Abe Patterson. Mid 1950's. Private collection.

"He accepted invitations to international sportsmen's shows and hobby shows in Indianapolis, Cleveland, Los Angeles, New York, Toronto, Vancouver, Mexico and Boston. Today his mail indicated orders with postmarks reading Denmark, Germany, Hollywood, London, Banff, Philadelphia, or just plain Pembroke. There is no priority. The millionaire waits his turn at the same modest shop on Murray Street."

Patterson passed away in 1969. The small workshop building adjacent to his house stood empty for several years until his widow decided that it should be torn down. She raised the matter with one of her sons, who completed the task as she had requested. Pat Patterson told me he regretted that the building had been demolished. "I would have

Front cover, *The Ottawa Evening Journal* in 1941 with photograph of Abe Patterson showing off a carving at a Boston trade show.

saved it," he said ruefully during our interview. "That was the building where my Dad carved so many things."

Given his output, promotional activity, and the fact that he was a professional woodcarver, it is not unreasonable to suggest that Abe Patterson was a successful commercial artist rather than a folk artist. On the other hand, he was self-taught and created works by hand that reflected the world around him or his vision of the past. His carvings exquisitely capture the subjects he wanted to depict including meticulous details. He challenged himself to create carvings in wood for extraordinary projects and he was dedicated to his art. Perhaps the type of artist he was is irrelevant and he is in a category all his own.

Fred Bailey (Shawville, Quebec)

Fred Bailey (1903 – 1998) of Shawville, Quebec, was an excellent wood carver. I came to know the retired carpenter's work in the late 1980s, when I purchased two of his carvings from Rick Huxtable. A few years ago, I visited Mr. Bailey's daughter near Shawville. She had been in touch with me after seeing one of her father's carving in an interview I did with Joel Haslam of CTV News.

I spent a pleasant hour with Nora Findlay, chatting and looking at the carvings she had in her possession. She estimated her father produced a total of about eighty carvings in a ten-to fifteen-year period. Most of them featured horses, which he loved.

She told me a touching story about how her father lost his 198-acre family farm in the Eastern Townships of Quebec. Down but not out, Mr. Bailey and his wife left and travelled to her hometown of Shawville, northwest of Ottawa, where they hoped to make a new start. Mr. Bailey's spirit was again tested when his horse was injured and had to be destroyed en route. Undeterred, Mr. Bailey and his wife travelled on to Shawville and successfully restarted their lives. He worked several jobs and finally settled on carpentry as his main occupation, one he would pursue for the rest of his working life.

While she had several examples of his work there that day, Nora was not interested in selling any of them. I was not surprised. If I were in her position, I would not sell them either. So, I had to satisfy myself with taking photographs.

Couple in a buggy, wood carving by Fred Bailey. Mid 1990's. Private collection.

A few weeks later, I was casually looking at Facebook and you can imagine my surprise when a terrific wood carving by Mr. Bailey turned up at the Elora Antique Show. Mr. Bailey's daughter had a similar piece in her collection—important information that allowed me to react quickly. I messaged Adrian Tinline who was exhibiting at the show and he purchased the piece on my behalf. Another dealer acquaintance who was also exhibiting at the show brought the carving back to Ottawa. It is called The Race and features a standardbred horse race with four colourful participants. It is dated 1974 and signed by the artist.

Mr. Bailey mounted all his pieces on short wood planks. On the edges of the plank, he would typically engrave a title, his name, and the year he created the work. He also made clear plexiglass cases to protect his works, and both the Bailey carvings I purchased still had their cases. The cases are easily dismantled by removing the small screws at each corner of the case.

Mr. Bailey's work exhibits the defining characteristics of excellent folk art: inspired carving, memories of days gone by, naïve yet charming execution, a strong sense of purpose, and confidence. It is not surprising that horses are featured in so many of his carvings, as these animals were an important part of his life and community.

Harness racing carving by Fred Bailey. Private collection.

The work of folk artists reflects the personality of the artist. An excellent piece of folk art informs the observer about the artist's way of life and their feelings toward their environment. Clearly, Fred Bailey accomplished this. His wood carvings successfully capture the mood and posture of animals in various settings, such as the racetrack, harvest time, and transportation. While folk art includes many crude examples of wood carving or items painted in a slap-dash manner, Mr. Bailey's work is characterized by an attention to detail, down to the harnesses, which he made from narrow strips of leather harvested from his wife's old purses.

I prefer folk art carvings that are finished with paint colours. For the most part, Mr. Bailey painted his, often in several different colours and with the utmost care. An exception is his many walking canes, which he finished in a clear coat of varnish.

Fred Bailey's wood carvings are bright and lively with a folk charm that elevates them above the average, making his work a joy to see and a pleasure to own.

Carp Station by Brian Hayes.

MEMORIES ON CANVAS:
THE ART OF BRIAN HAYES

I do not typically purchase modern works of folk art. Most of the pieces in my collection date from before 1970, many much earlier than that. I do make the occasional exception, and the folk art paintings of the late Brian Hayes (1963 – 2010) are a case in point.

Brian Hayes was born in Leamington, Ontario to Jack and Yvonne Hayes. He was a younger brother to John Hayes. Like many folk artists, Brian was completely self-taught.

His father and brother, John, are both long-time members of the Bytown Antique and Bottle Club. Until her death, Yvonne was also a dedicated member. Some years ago, Jack graciously toured me through his home and showed me his wonderful collection of antiques and merchant stoneware. During the visit, I first saw Brian Hayes' paintings and was immediately impressed. His work clearly shows a confident and meticulous artist. When I inquired about purchasing some pieces, Jack made several paintings available to me.

After living with Brian Hayes' paintings for a few years, I am convinced he was a truly gifted folk artist. His quality approaches that of William Kurelek (1927 – 1977), the eccentric Canadian painter who painted, among other subjects, colourful and detailed scenes of Depression-era farm life in western Canada.

Hayes' work also reminds me of E. J. Hughes (1913 – 2007), the British Columbia painter who, to quote his web site, "painted the small moments of daily life with a rare clarity and vividness".

Brian Hayes focused his work on times past and his paintings capture local Ottawa valley towns like Carp, Almonte, and Pakenham. Some images are from the 1960s; others are scenes as he imagined they would have been in the late 1800s or early 1900s. All feature heritage buildings and structures of the time, many of which are no longer standing.

The town of Pakenham, Ontario, an early painting by Brian Hayes, about 1982. Private collection.

According to Jack, his son's aptitude for drawing and painting emerged at about twenty years of age. The earliest of his paintings that Jack has in his collection is a small watercolour that depicts the village of Pakenham in Lanark County, Ontario. It is dated 1985, when the artist would have been twenty-two.

The Pakenham village scene has many of the characteristics that would continue to show up in Hayes' paintings for the rest of his life. He was fascinated with details and his work is filled with meticulous characteristics of small-town life—the people, the animals, and especially the heritage buildings. His Pakenham scene includes the historic five-span stone bridge that crosses the Mississippi River, plus a large stone industrial building and several houses along the main street of the village.

Folk artists often like to provide as much information as possible in their work. Brian's painting brims with details, some obvious, others subtle. If he included a stone building from the mid 19th-century in a painting, he would have a team of horses harnessed to a wagon standing in the lane beside it. A vintage automotive garage built from cinder blocks around 1920 would include a perfectly detailed vehicle of that era waiting for fuel. The gas pump, of course, would be one of the early gravity-fed types with the clear glass cylinder, used prior to electric pumps, that showed how much gas was being delivered into the vehicle.

The first of Hayes' paintings I purchased depicts a scene in the village of Carp, Ontario, about twenty miles west of downtown Ottawa, where he lived for a period of time. The village takes its name from the Carp River, which runs through it. The main street was once part of the Trans-Canada Highway but was bypassed by a new highway in later years. The artist depicts the village as it was in the mid-1960s. As such, it is a memory painting, a popular idiom for folk artists.

IGA in the Village of Carp by Brian Hayes, 2002. Author's collection.

He chose to paint a tranquil summer scene. In it, a young man casually strolls along the sidewalk past the IGA Supermarket. To the left is a little building housing a barber shop. An impressive two-storey home is on the right. A vintage half-ton truck is parked on the street, the name R. W. Moore's Grocery, clearly visible on the driver's door. The buildings are backed by clusters of deciduous spruce and white pine trees. Several clouds trundle across an otherwise blue summer sky.

Looking more closely at the painting, one sees further details. The shingles of the home are painted individually, as are the red bricks in the two chimneys. Two iron lightning rods adorn the roof of the home, complete with opaque glass tops. A tubular aluminum garden chair with plastic interwoven fabric, circa 1960s, sits on the front porch. A much older plank-seated country chair is to the left of it.

Most artists would not have included a hydro pole directly in the middle of the painting, but Hayes did. He also included the top portion of a hydro pole visible behind the store, its horizontal trusses adorned with glass insulators. (Hayes' father and brother are keen collectors of insulators.) The GMC truck's license plate includes the number 65, which perhaps subtly dates the painting to the mid-1960s era.

Detail from the Carp IGA painting by Brian Hayes.

Brian Hayes obviously took precious effort on the windows of the IGA, which include signs for "Borden's Milk" and "Fresh Pork Chops". He was also careful to paint each individual cinder block in the store's façade. A sandwich board advertising ice cream for sale sits on the sidewalk, partially obscured by the truck. He even depicted the fronts of the shops across the street reflected in the IGA store windows.

Like many folk artists, Brian Hayes had to deal with the demands of perspective and scale. While he succeeds for the most part, the Milano barber shop is unrealistically small. The angled side of the grocery store seems inconsistent with those of the other two buildings in the painting (three buildings if you include the garage behind the store). It is possible that he intentionally flattened the perspective of his painting, a technique also used by E.J. Hughes and others, because it allowed the artist to include more objects. If a folk artist is not aware of the rules of perspective or chooses to ignore them, the result still satisfies them because there is more detail in the work.

Brian Hayes' parents owned the Pakenham General Store from 1981 to 1987. (Today, the business is 180 years old and still operating as a general store in the same heritage building.) Jack and Yvonne were avid collectors of many things, including 19th-century decorated merchant stoneware. They would frequently set up a booth at the Stittsville Flea Market to sell antiques and collectibles. Their son would often set up, too, and sell various items he had picked up during the week. Like his mother, father, and brother John, he was a collector and knew the value of items and what would sell at the flea market.

According to Jack, his son was a quiet individual with many friends, observant, and a good listener. When he was not painting, he maintained an exceptional garden in the backyard of the house where he lived.

I have other works by Brian Hayes. One is a painting of a Newfoundland outport—he once traveled to the Atlantic province with his father. The painting depicts part of a fishing village with a fishing trawler, the NFLD ROSE, her captain at the wheel steering between buoys toward the dock. In this work, Brian focused on subtle but important details. The horizontal green wood siding on the houses is carefully painted. The bricks of a chimney on one of the houses are each outlined individually. A man waits on the dock, his gaze fixed on the incoming trawler, perhaps ready to throw a line to the boat. Several buildings are perched on shore, including two houses and several sheds. Men are busy on shore with their daily tasks. Despite the grey skies, washing is hanging on the line to dry at one house. The painting is again strongly reminiscent of the work of William Kuralek and E.J. Hughes.

Newfoundland outport painted by Brian Hayes 2001. Author's collection.

Over time, Brian Hayes' reputation as an artist grew. He set up a small gallery in a house in Carp and his paintings were reproduced both as prints and greeting cards. His family hoped that his career as an artist would continue to blossom and provide him with a modest but steady income, and he was well on his way to achieving that goal. A high point came when he was featured on Regional Contact, a long-running, popular CTV television show watched throughout the Ottawa Valley and Eastern Ontario. Joel Haslam of CTV interviewed Hayes for the segment.

Unfortunately, Brian Hayes had health issues and died suddenly of a heart attack in 2010, at the age of forty-seven. We can only wonder at the art that this talented, quiet young man might have produced had he lived a longer life. Collectors like me thankfully treasure what we do have of his work.

Brian Hayes holding one of his artworks. Private collection.

Folk art winter scene from Westport, Ontario, about 1900. Now in a private collection.

The Art of the Chase

I was running late, but confident I would get to the auction hall in time. After all, the piece of folk art I was interested in would not come up for sale, I thought, until well into the evening. It was a carving by the late Odessa Belisle of St. Antoine, Quebec, depicting a farmer working a field behind a pair of oxen. The carving was nicely done, and more importantly to me, was painted in various colours, which added to its appeal.

I arrived at the hall, parked, and hustled into the auction room. "Damn it!" I cursed under my breath when I saw the auctioneer's helpers already at the back of the room holding up items for sale. They were well past the folk art carving I had hoped to bid on. A quick conversation with a dealer friend sitting at the side of the room confirmed my fears. And to add insult to injury—he himself had bought it!

A few days after that auction sale, I could not stop thinking about the Belisle carving and I called the friend who had bought it. We negotiated a price, which also included some minor repairs, and a few days later, I happily took possession of this excellent piece of Canadian folk art. He even called me a few weeks later to tell me he had another piece by Odessa Belisle, and I added that carving to my collection, as well.

In truth, I have a love/hate relationship with auctions. It is exciting to see quality objects at an auction and it is painful knowing you will have to bid against often stiff competition to win the item or items of your desire. The situation is made even more intense now that auctioneers have taken their sales to the Internet. Instead of bidding against the collectors and dealers in your community, you may now well be bidding against someone halfway around the world!

My interest in the field of folk art was first piqued by Blake McKendry's book, *Folk Art, Primitive and Naïve Art in Canada.* Some years earlier, spurred on by an interest in family history, I had started to collect country furniture.

Wood carving by Odessa Belisle. Mid 1960s. Author's collection.

McKendry's book opened my eyes to the complementary field of folk art.

As I discovered, there are two avenues of folk art open to collectors: traditional and contemporary. I was aware of traditional folk art because it was closely aligned with antique country items. However, because it combines age with artistic expression, traditional folk art is more expensive than contemporary. For a new collector like myself at the time, contemporary folk art offered a field of collecting that was relatively new and affordable.

As the name implies, folk art is art created by individuals who typically have no formal training. They simply pick up a paint brush, a carving knife, or sewing needle and start to create. Collectors are drawn to folk art because of the naïve charm of the works.

Mr. McKendry's book alerted me to folk artists from Eastern Ontario, like Arthur Sauvé of Maxville, and I began to search for their works. It was not long before I ranged further afield and began collecting the work of maritime artists like Joe Norris and Maud Lewis.

Painting by Maud Lewis. Early 1960s. Author's collection.

Travelling about Eastern Ontario, I also came across undiscovered folk artists and added their works to my collection. Some folk artists never exhibit their work, storing it away in closets and basements. They often think that their work is not good enough to be seen in public and certainly not good enough to be sold. Every once in a while, you come across these hidden works—an exciting moment for a folk art collector!

In a good piece of folk art, the artist exhibits a strong command of their subject despite having no formal training. There is a confidence and a notable assuredness to the work. While the artist may not know the rules of perspective or composition, it is not a limitation. A good folk artist earnestly accomplishes what they set out to do, be it a painting, a quilt, a hooked mat, or a wood carving.

Likewise, you do not have to be a student of art or an expert to appreciate folk art. It speaks to you directly, spontaneously, with charm and innocence.

In today's market, contemporary folk art is still, with some exceptions, quite affordable. Collectors can choose to focus on paintings, textiles, carvings, metalwork, or works by particular artists. That is the nice thing about the folk art field: it is broad and deep.

An exceptional piece of folk art can turn up just about anywhere. Certainly, you will see folk art in antique shops and at auctions, but I have also purchased great examples of folk art at garage sales, flea markets, estate sales, church bazaars, and rummage sales. You never know where the next exciting piece will turn up, and that is part of its magic, too.

For today's folk art collectors, there are several excellent books on the subject. *Canadian Folk Art to 1950,* by John A. Fleming and Michael J. Rowan, is the most recent. This superb book should be kept close at hand by all folk art collectors.

Over the years, I have developed a mental checklist against which I judge all pieces that come to my attention. If a piece of folk art meets all or most these criteria, I will consider it regardless of age:

- appealing subject matter
- use of colour
- naïve yet confident execution
- good condition
- age

I recently found three terrific folk art paintings by a Quebec artist that were created in the year 2000. Would I have preferred that they were older? Yes. But their recent creation does not, for me, detract from their appeal as works of folk art, although it may for other collectors.

As I see it, superb folk art is difficult enough to find without adding further constraints. After all, collecting is about the anticipation, the hunt, *and* the acquisition. If I restrict my criteria too tightly, I will not be able to collect as much.

My criteria are likely different from yours and from that of other collectors. Understanding your preferences and priorities is an important aspect of collecting.

Some people collect only "traditional" folk art, meaning, for the most part, items that are 100 years old and more. Others may collect items that have age but are not antique per se. We've all seen stunning examples of folk art that date to the 1920s, '30s, and later.

Exquisite small wooden bible box used to store prayer books for the journey to Sunday church. It is festooned with decorative chip carving and dated 1884 on the reverse side. Private collection.

Painted crucifix wood carving by Arthur Sauvé, Maxville, Ontario, c. 1955. Private collection.

As indicated by their book title, authors Fleming and Rowan chose a creation cut-off date of 1950 to frame the wonderful items featured in their book. By virtue of that deadline, works by noted Canadian folk artists such as Maud Lewis and Joe Norris are excluded.

While the 1950 deadline may seem arbitrary, Michael Rowan told me, during a brief conversation, that the year was chosen because television had not yet been invented—television would likely have influenced the artists and the subjects they chose. The year 1950 also served a practical purpose by allowing the authors to contain the scope of the book. Even so, this comprehensive publication includes several hundred items, many of which have national cultural significance.

Like many collectibles, folk art has become so popular that inferior examples are prevalent in the market. I see all kinds of pieces that have poor form, crude execution, and which are visually unpleasant or plain ugly. These are not the type of pieces I want in my collection. If you are going to collect folk art, I suggest you should avoid these items too. With a seemingly endless number of vendors needing a constant supply of stock, if an item even faintly resembles something "folky" it will find its way onto the market.

The best collectors I know, whether they focus on antiques, folk art, nostalgia, mid-century modern, or other categories, all operate from a sound base of knowledge. They have reference libraries and they network with other collectors and dealers. They are constantly learning and refining the skills of successful collecting.

Of course you can bypass all of that and simply spend your way to a collection. But I feel we have more than enough of that in modern life, rushing back and forth, trying to keep up with the demands of work, family, and bills while trying to put something aside for retirement.

Collecting should be an oasis, removed from everyday pressures and demands. Along with the excitement of the hunt and the acquisition of important objects, collecting should create space for contemplation, research, education, and enhanced understanding of the world around us. In short, it should enrich our lives.

When I look at a piece of folk art, or any art for that matter, I observe both the object and the personality of the artist. The art reflects the artist's life and what is important to them. Brilliantly executed folk art, especially traditional folk art, has a palpable grace, dignity, and charm.

Any exceptional art is not easy to find, and that makes collecting interesting and enticing. One never knows what a day or week of hunting will produce. Sure, the results can be frustrating and discouraging. Those times make the wonderful moments much richer. Seemingly out of nowhere—in an antique shop, a market, the back of a picker's truck, at a rummage sale, or a local auction—there it is, your next big find: the item that checks all the boxes on your mental list. Those are the moments that keep us all going and fuel the stories we tell for years to come.

As I write this, it is early morning on a Saturday. I am in my office surrounded by many things that I found and purchased last summer, before COVID-19. Looking at each one, I recall the excitement and the pleasure of acquiring a superb example of folk art. I want to experience that feeling again and again. Few things in life that offer that kind of return.

I missed buying this impressive hanging cupboard over 20 years ago. I was the underbidder again this year but managed to buy the piece after the sale. Author's collection.

Beyond the Surface: Evaluating Country Furniture

Ideally, the advanced collector of country furniture wants an original surface, meaning the surface that the cabinetmaker put on the piece when they finished it. Typical finishes on country furniture include paint, stain, varnish, or a combination of these. In some cases, as with harvest tables or kitchen tables, the tops were left without a finish because food was often prepared on them. Collectors occasionally come across a piece of furniture that was never painted or varnished, but the bulk of furniture items had some sort of finish coat applied.

There is no getting around it: if you are looking for antique furniture, be prepared to see a lot of the colour brown. In the 19th century, brown was popular likely because cabinet makers were trying to make the furniture look like, well, brown furniture—as if it were made from desirable woods. While thousands of items were made from mahogany, walnut, and cherry, outside of city centres, white pine, butternut, and basswood were more commonly available. Cabinetmakers or anyone adept with hand tools could construct a piece of furniture and add a paint finish that made it look like a more expensive wood.

Washstand of unknown origin found in original painted condition. Remarkably, the narrow legs have never been broken. Pine, c. 1850. Author's collection.

Occasionally, furniture was painted in colours like blue, green, yellow, red, and so on. Because there were fewer of these pieces, they have a higher market value. If you see an original colour of green or blue on a piece of Canadian antique country furniture, pay attention—it is a rare treat to see such a thing, let alone to buy it.

It is also rare to find antiques in original surface only, and more common to find them with additional layers of paint or varnish added to freshen them up them over the years. Provided that the original finish is still under there—that the piece has not been stripped—it is often possible to restore it to its original surface by removing the later layers of paint or varnish. While

A chimney cupboard from Lanark County scraped to original green paint. Pine, forged nails, c. 1830. Author's collection.

I have successfully restored several items in our collection, I don't hesitate to use a professional restoration expert for more difficult situations.

Cabinet makers would sometimes simulate more expensive woods by first painting the piece a dark red then adding stripes of wavy black paint over top to simulate the look of mahogany. Figured maple and quarter-cut oak was also simulated in this manner. These surfaces are usually original but were also added later. Faux finishes are rare and sought after.

Overpaint refers to paint applied over top of an original finish. It reduces the value of an antique, but less so on a piece that has excellent form and provenance. Overpaint can be removed such that the original painted surface is revealed and preserved. Some collectors prefer, on the advice of restoration specialists, to leave the item in the overpaint, called *as-found*.

Nicks, scratches, wear, and other visual signs of age on the finish that occur over time comprise is called *patina*. This is the visual legacy of a piece of antique furniture and advanced collectors focus their collecting on items with patinated original finish because the entire history of the piece is represented on that surface.

Over the years, something wonderful happens to paint on, say, a pine cupboard door. The colour becomes richer and warmer. Some paint surfaces crackle over time. Paint may be completely worn off in areas where hands and fingers have repeatedly touched drawer pulls and the edges of doors. Old pine becomes smooth to the touch. These are the signs of patina and age that advanced collectors desire.

You may encounter a piece of antique furniture that has a poor surface or no surface (meaning that it has been stripped of all finish down to bare wood) and poor form. Many advanced collectors shy away from stripped and refinished furniture, especially if the piece has average or poor form. Many stellar pieces of refinished Canadian furniture are available with terrific age, form, and condition. In some cases, collectors will have an antique repainted in a colour that looks like the original.

An example of wear on antique furniture.

Time, use, and the environment can all be hard on an antique. Left in a dry environment to perform the functions for which it was originally intended, a piece of country furniture can last indefinitely. Many pieces, however, are repurposed for tougher tasks and placed in harsher situations where, over time, their condition deteriorates to a point where there is nothing left worth saving. I have seen many once-beautiful cupboards that have been cut in half, their doors removed and thrown away, cornices and bracket bases lopped off, or with entire sections removed and missing. Often, these pieces end up as miscellaneous storage containers in basements, garages, and sheds.

On several occasions, I have tried to buy and save country furniture from overly damp basements and other negative situations, but the owner would not sell at any price. On those days, I consoled myself by obtaining the owner's permission to at least put the piece up on risers away from a damp floor. Other times, I have managed to buy a piece of country furniture and save it from further neglect.

It can be exciting to find sections of the same piece of furniture that have been separated, sometimes for decades, and bring them back together as the one piece they were intended to be. My friend, Rick Huxtable, of Huxtable Antiques, once found the base of an impressive pine cupboard in the Ottawa Valley. Flat-to-the-

This cupboard required repairs to the bottom and top right cornice return. Areas of the repairs were then colour matched. Author's collection.

wall cupboards were often made in two pieces, a top section and a bottom section, while others were made as a single piece of furniture. The cupboard Rick found was in original paint and featured raised panels in the doors and on its sides. Raised panels, as the name suggests, are typically rectangular pieces of wood that form the central part of a door or other flat surface and they are rare in country furniture.

Rick shrewdly thought that the top half of the cupboard, if it still existed, might have been moved to a neighbouring farm. He proceeded to knock on every nearby farmhouse door along that concession road. At one farm, about a mile away, he found the top half of the cupboard in a carriage shed. It was the same colour and had the same raised panels. Fortunately, he was able to buy both pieces and reunite this unique Ottawa Valley antique.

Rick Huxtable found the base of this heavily panelled cupboard in one location and the top half at a farm a mile away. Quebec, pine, c. 1850. Private collection.

While the surface of an antique is important, other factors are also at play, such as form (design) and condition. In a perfect world, the antique you are considering adding to your collection should score high marks on all three: surface, form, and condition. An antique with a great original surface and some weak points in the design might still be worth adding to a collection if it is in excellent condition. After all, some of the design and construction features are beneath the surface and not initially visible to the observer.

If a glazed cupboard has a small, unattractive cornice or a simple base moulding instead of a nice bracket base with a cut-out, those deficiencies may be overlooked because of a wonderful original surface. By contrast, a piece with terrific form and acceptable surface in poor condition—for example, if a substantial portion of the piece is missing or rotting away—probably cannot be redeemed.

Some condition problems can be addressed through restoration but doing so can impact the integrity of the piece. Many collectors will reject an antique out of hand if it has had more than a minimal amount of restoration. I tend to accept more restoration than the average collector simply because I like to see country furniture rescued and restored. I do not buy pieces that have been repurposed because of damage. Collectors have to be cautious because some 19th-century cupboards were "built-ins"—that is, attached directly to the walls or corners of a room. Often, these pieces are removed and altered to appear as a stand-alone cupboard.

Two other factors to consider are age and provenance. Age is important because, as antique collectors, we want to find objects that are old, and the older the better. Sometimes, we will compromise on age if the surface, form, and condition of a piece are of a high standard. Some collectors use 1900 as the dividing line of their collections: any object after that date will have to score high marks on all other factors to be acceptable to them as an antique. Other collectors prefer an earlier date as their cut off point, pre-1870, for example.

When the advanced collector or dealer approaches a piece of antique furniture, they evaluate it on all five factors: surface, form, condition, age, and provenance. It is rare indeed to find an antique that performs well in all these categories. More common are pieces that register well on some factors but not in others. Each collector must balance these factors and make an assessment of where the piece ranks on their personal scale.

Of course, price comes into the mix, too. Typically, if a piece scores high in all categories, the price will reflect that and a collector may have to stretch their budget to make the purchase. For a piece that is off-the-charts excellent, the price is just about anything the vendor wishes to place on it.

With experience, you will be able to look at a piece and make your first impression in moments. Then, assuming you have the time and the inclination, you can take a long second look and inspect the piece more carefully.

There is an old saying among pickers that "the back never lies". Always look at the back of a piece of furniture because it may reveal issues you do not see from the front. Also carefully inspect the top, sides, and bottom. Be on the lookout for inconsistencies: Are feet missing? Are the nails and fasteners all consistent? Are the saw marks the same? Is the wear on the paint where it should be? Have any new parts been added?

The detailed inspection will either confirm or adjust your initial reaction as you evaluate, colour, surface, form, condition, age and provenance. Certain things can trip up a collector: fakes, forgeries, imports, repurposed pieces, and repainted items, to name a few. We all make mistakes and that is why it is important to keep your guard up. With experience, you will catch most inconsistencies during an inspection. Asking for a second opinion is always a good idea as another collector might see things about a piece that you have missed.

Surface carving and decoration on country furniture are extremely rare features with a few exceptions. For example, Wilno blanket boxes are found with hand-painted floral decorations on the front panels. Accessories like wall boxes and other small containers are more likely to feature hand carving and decoration—but even these are rare items and, because they include artistic details, they are highly valued and priced accordingly. Even with these small items, you should still assess them against all the criteria described earlier.

Collecting Canadian antique country furniture is a terrific pastime that can be both exciting and rewarding. To get the most from it, be prepared and knowledgeable—two characteristics of a collector that take time to develop. But there is no hurry and the learning itself is pleasurable and will make your discoveries and purchases that much more enjoyable.

Miniature chest of drawers in pine, original vanish, signed and dated 1917. Author's collection.

The Beauty of Small: Salesman's Samples, Children's Furniture, and Gifts from the Heart

Small-scale furniture, especially in the realm of country furniture, is a fascinating area of collecting with many advantages. You will likely never have an issue with literally fitting a piece into your collection. As the collection grows, you do not need much space, just an efficient method of displaying the objects you have found. The pieces look neat in their own dedicated showcase or they can grace the tops of their full-scale cousins: cupboards, armoires, tables, and chests of drawers.

Small-scale furniture items are small but not miniature. Collectors often refer to small-scale items as salesman samples. These pieces were made to be transported from farm to farm, home to home, allowing a vendor to demonstrate the talents of the cabinetmaker and show customers exactly what they could expect from the maker. Although the term salesman sample is used by collectors almost generically to describe a range of small furniture pieces, clearly many items were made by woodworkers for children to enjoy as toys and were never intended to serve as samples of anything.

On a trip to Toronto to visit my sister, Sharon Colle, Joan and I stopped at a consignment store where we had found good things in the past. Wandering through the store, I came across a small chest of drawers that was substantially smaller than one made for a child. Its dimensions were 18" high, 14" wide, and 10" deep. It had features such as a moulding around one of the drawer fronts, split columns applied to the front vertical edges, and turned feet. It even had two false drawers! Another attractive detail was that it was in original finish—a dark brown, almost black, paint. Made entirely of pine

Salesman sample, chest of drawers, pine, about 1870 in original paint, from Atlantic Canada. Author's collection.

and joined with square nails, its date of creation must have been about 1870. It was a marvel that something that size survived 150 years completely intact. All the drawer pulls were there, all the drawers were in good working condition, and even the little turned feet were still firmly in place.

Whoever did the assessment for the consignment store knew that the chest had value, but the price had been reduced to $310. I wasted little time carrying it to the front desk, paying, and taking that beauty to the car. That was fifteen years ago, and we treasure it to this day.

To evaluate quality in salesman samples or miniature furniture, a collector should use the same checklist of factors as that of full-size pieces: surface, form, condition, age, and provenance. Items lose points for being overpainted, made after 1900, not having an interesting form, or coming with little or no information about their lineage.

Do not assume that the whimsy of small-scale furniture means these pieces lack the sophistication of full-size pieces. Many cabinetmakers poured considerable talent into making these pieces and the attention to detail on some of them is amazing. Rather, the whimsy of small bestows an extra value on these little fellows. They are notorious for causing even the

Small document box with raised panel on lid. Made entirely of solid birds eye maple. Made about 1850 in the Ottawa Valley. Private collection.

sternest collector to smile upon seeing them.

Small-scale furniture is not difficult to find. Perhaps because of their diminutive size, their rate of survival is better. They get tucked away in closets and cupboards, not carried into damp basements and old barns to serve extended duty as repositories for preserves and paint cans.

Being small in scale does not mean the value of these pieces are less than their full-size cousins. In fact, salesman samples can be worth considerably more, with prices for excellent pieces reaching up to and beyond $2,000. It is also possible to find nice examples of small-scale furniture in the $500 range. Every once and a while, though, you will want to step up and pay the premium for a signature piece to anchor your collection.

Furniture made for children, like a child's chest of drawers or a small cupboard, is often more desirable than large sizes of the same type of furniture. Toward the end of the 19th century, rooms in houses were a generous size and ceilings were often ten to twelve feet high. Hence, cabinetmakers of the time built furniture to fit, and it is not uncommon for pickers to come across cupboards over eight feet high and five feet wide. Harvest tables have been found at eight, ten, and even twelve feet in length. At a certain point, furniture can simply become too big for most potential buyers.

Small-scale furniture and salesman samples may turn up just about anywhere. Antique shows, flea markets, garage and estate sales, the Internet, church bazaars—all these sources may produce a great find. You must be on your toes and out there searching—and that is what collecting is all about.

Found in Ottawa, this miniature blanket chest likely came from Quebec. Original colour, minor repairs, pine, c. 1850. Author's collection.

Small furniture is very functional. Collectors use these pieces to store precious items like jewelry. It is also fun to display them beside life-size furniture, where they can quickly become the highlight of a conversation.

On occasion, makers would sign a drawer bottom with their name. To discover a penciled note written 100 years ago on the back of a little antique dresser is a moving experience, a portal into the mind and heart of the individual who made the item and signed it.

Many years ago, at an antique show in Toronto, I purchased a tiny chest of drawers in original paint for just $50. It had original, oversized drawer pulls and a wonderful backsplash. Looking at the piece more closely, I found an inscription on the bottom of one of the drawers. There, in pencil, were the words: "Made for Phyllis, Christmas 1904".

Very few antiques are signed, let alone dated. I have been collecting for forty years and can count on two hands the number of signed and dated pieces I have found. Signed pieces are quite often smaller and given as gifts.

I purchased another signed item in 2019 at a yard sale in the west-end of Ottawa where items were spread out on a tarp on the front lawn. I saw a small wooden trinket box with its front-edge trim missing. The little box was made of oak with walnut trim and looked a bit worse for wear. It was about ten inches long, five inches deep, and four inches high. In original

A pine miniature chest of drawers with scalloped backboard, two drawers, and original brass pulls. Found in Toronto, original paint and dated 1904. Author's collection.

varnish, it was unremarkable except for one thing: an inscription on the interior, written in somewhat faded pencil: "Made and given to Jessie M. Shouldice by her father John F. Shouldice, Xmas 1898".

I posted a photo and description of the trinket box on Facebook. Bob and Linda Henderson of Markham, Ontario did some research on the Shouldice

The Shouldice trinket box, oak with walnut trim, original varnish. Found in Ottawa, signed and dated 1898. Authors collection.

The inscription reads: *"Made and given to Jessie M. Shouldice by her father John F. Shouldice, Xmas 1898."*

name and wrote asking if the "G" might in fact be an "F". On closer inspection, I found that it was. Linda's research had uncovered a John F. Shouldice in the 1881 and 1891 Ottawa Census (Wellington Ward). Mr. Shouldice was a "mill man" born 1839 in Ontario and had a daughter, Jessie M., born in 1876. She would have been twenty-two years old when her father crafted the box and gifted it to her in 1898.

Soon, however, another sleuth came forward.

I wrote an article about the little box for *Canadian Antiques & Vintage* magazine. Not long after the article appeared, I received an email from Tyler Shouldice—the great-great grandson of John F. Shouldice. Tyler surmised that the box was most likely made at 257 Bronson Avenue in Ottawa, as opposed to Dunrobin about twenty miles west of Ottawa as I had suggested in the magazine article. Tyler also suspected it was kept in Jessie's possession throughout her entire lifetime and may well have been presented to her at the last Christmas that the family were together under one roof. Best of all, Tyler sent along a photo of his great-great grandfather, the box's maker.

The Shouldice trinket box is not a valuable antique. Less than a hundred dollars would likely buy it any day of the week. It does not boast elaborate details in its construction—it has no dovetailed joints, cut-outs, bracket base, nor any fancy original paint with flowers or hearts. What it does have, however, is provenance, thanks to John F. Shouldice penciling that inscription onto the bottom of the box. Because of that, we know it

John F. Shouldice.

is 121 years old, made in Ottawa, and a symbol of a mill-man's love for his daughter, Jessie. In my books, that makes it a most valuable object indeed.

As a rule of thumb, small is always good in antiques and that is true of small-scale furniture, too. Often overlooked, these little creations continue to create joy and fascination for all who collect them.

Photo from Bytown Antique and Bottle Club 2017 calendar. The tiger maple table and the oil lamps are from private collections.

16
A Stroll Through the Woods

A friend and fellow antique collector recently commented online that he was going to learn to recognize the different types of wood used by cabinetmakers. It is a useful skill to develop for any collector of things made of wood. While I did not intentionally make the decision to learn about wood species, I have gradually come to a point where I can recognize most of the woods used in the making of North American antique country furniture. Sometimes, you will not be able to identify a particular species of wood, but those are species you will likely not see very often—apple and olive wood are good examples, but these species are used most often as decorative inlays on more formal furniture and not in country furniture.

For a collector, identifying the wood goes hand-in-hand with assessing and understanding the techniques used to construct a piece of furniture. Especially with country furniture, the entire piece may be made of pine—but you will frequently discover that, along with the pine, the maker used basswood, birch, maple, cherry, butternut, etc. Recognizing the various woods with which a piece is made brings a sense of personal satisfaction and it also gives a collector a competitive advantage. Combined knowledge of wood species, furniture styles, design features, and construction techniques is the complete mental tool kit for understanding antique furniture and wooden accessories.

Wood species indicates the origin of a piece of furniture. For example, the species most often used in North American antique furniture include pine, oak, ash, butternut, elm, basswood, maple (plain and figured), walnut, cherry, birch, mahogany, and poplar. Occasionally, you will see cedar and it is often confused with pine.

Photo of the underside of a table drawer made from pine. Note the parallel lines in the grain on the bottom and sides of the drawer, a characteristic of white pine. Table is mid 1850's from the Ottawa Valley. Author's collection.

Cabinet makers frequently made the panels of cupboard doors from basswood because it resists shrinking and cracking over time. Poplar has a telltale faint green tinge to it and was popular with cabinet makers in the U.S. as a secondary wood, but much less so in Canada. So, if you see poplar used for drawer sides or bottoms, you can be reasonably sure the piece originated south of the border. Extensive use of elm can indicate a piece imported from England.

If you collect country furniture, like me, your focus will be on pine, although basswood and butternut were frequently used, too. Walnut, cherry, mahogany, and figured maple were used more in formal furniture.

Furniture made from figured maple is either tiger maple (the grain has vivid stripes that contrast with the normal appearance of the grain) or bird's-eye maple (the grain features tiny circles). Antique maple furniture has a loyal following of collectors, and prices for these pieces remain consistently high.

The late Donald Blake Webster, then Curator of the Canadiana Department at the Royal Ontario Museum, offered his opinion on the importance of knowing the various woods used in Canadian furniture:

Close up of figured maple drawer fronts from a chest of drawers found in Eastern Ontario. c. 1870. Author's collection.

"Wood identification is perhaps the most important factor in identifying early Canadian furniture. The hardwoods used—mahogany, native birch, cherry, maple, walnut and butternut, are generally combined with pine as a secondary wood. In English furniture, the secondary wood was very often oak, which is almost never used in Canadian furniture. American furniture, however, also used secondary pine, but this was commonly combined with other secondary woods. In Canadian furniture, pine was generally used alone.

"In Ontario, for example, bird's-eye or curly maple combined with cherry was extremely common. Ontario is also the only province where walnut grows natively."

The wood used to make a piece of antique furniture is one factor in the assessment process. How that wood is joined in the making of the piece, where it is featured in the piece, and the overall present condition of the item are also important.

White pine was the wood of choice for most cabinetmakers. However, they would frequently disguise pine by painting and varnishing it to look like mahogany, a more expensive species. Some collectors favour furniture with faux finishes, pieces are made of softwood and finished to look like exotic species.

Although the varnish has darkened considerably over the last 100 years, this side table from Kemptville, Ontario features a bird's eye maple drawer front with flame birch used in the top and sides. The pattern of the flame birch can be seen directly above the drawer. c. 1860. Author's collection and previously part of the Ken Lawless collection.

Recognizing white pine signals that a piece was likely made in North America, although, in the last twenty-five years, antique pine furniture made in Britain was imported by many shop owners. Most of this furniture has been stripped to a bleached, dry appearance and once you have seen a few of these pieces, you will recognize them instantly.

In the last twenty-five years or so, European antique country furniture began to appear in the market here and in the U.S. made of softwood and also painted with elaborate decorations. From a collecting standpoint, these pieces present a further level of complexity for the new collector to navigate. As some dealers have proven, there is a ready market for this material in Canada. Should your need be purely decorative, these pieces might satisfy; however, do not believe anyone who tells you they were made in North America.

If your focus is Canadian country antique furniture, you will want to train yourself to recognize the differences between what was made here and what was made in Europe. The vibrant, deep colours and floral decorations that frequently characterize European antique imports are rarely seen on Canadian pieces. Subtle differences in smaller pieces like spice cabinets and wall boxes are easy to spot with experience. Different hardware and fasteners are important indicators of European origin and unlike anything that was made here. The round nails used to join the lumber often have a hatch mark pattern on the head of the nail, another sign that the piece has a European origin.

A variety of books available on the topic of antique furniture and furniture restoration can help guide a new collector. *The Furniture Doctor*, by George Grotz, is a great place to start and includes a good chapter on wood species in antique furniture making.

When you are considering a piece of antique furniture, it may seem a lot to ask a dealer to allow you to see all four sides of the piece, but the request should not come as a surprise to them. I would be concerned and would likely walk away if a dealer did not let me inspect every aspect of a piece, and assist me in doing so. On occasion such an examination will reveal characteristics about a furniture item of which even the dealer was unaware.

17

EARLY OTTAWA ANTIQUE DEALERS, MURRAY AND MARY COPELAND

Dr. Murray Copeland (1928 – 2006) and is wife, Mary Copeland (1932 – 2007) had a long career as antique dealers in the Ottawa area, stretching back to the 1960s. They were contemporaries of the McKendrys (Chapter 10) and Philip and Marg Shackleton (Chapter 21). These three couples were among the first collectors and dealers of Canadian antiques in the Ottawa area. In fact, as long-time collector, Steve Cunliffe, described it, there were so few collectors at that time that this trio would often sell objects to one another. For some time, especially during the winter months, that was the extent of their business.

Mrs. Copeland held a B.A. from Flint University and Dr. Copeland had a distinguished career as a paleontologist with the Geological Survey of Canada. Like the McKendrys, the Copelands made many buying trips into Quebec and Atlantic Canada. They hunted not only for superior examples of country furniture, but also for fine antiques made by skilled provincial cabinet makers.

The Copelands operated an antique store

Interior of the Copeland's Antiques shop, March Corners about 1970.

from what was once McMurtry's General Store, located at the corner of Old Highway 17 and Klondike Road in March Township, a few miles west of Ottawa. The building was built in the 1850s as a private home then evolved into a general store and post office.

The McMurtry General Store, March Corners, present day.

A small crock from a competing outlet, the Armstrong General Store in March Corners. Private collection.

Prior to opening the store, the Copelands sold antiques from their home on Hare Avenue in Ottawa's west end. She stripped the furniture behind the garage and he carried out various small repairs and did the refinishing of the antique furniture. In the 1960s, stripping and refinishing painted pine furniture was a standard practice among dealers. At the time, very few individuals appreciated the look and feel of an original surface. Over time, collectors and dealers began to appreciate original surfaces and many stopped stripping and refinishing items. Still, there are countless situations where removing the paint and refinishing is the only reasonable option. Thousands of interesting pieces of early Canadian furniture survive to this day in collections in refinished condition and because of their form and age are still highly desirable antiques.

The Copeland's daughter, Susan, often accompanied her parents on buying trips. She has vivid memories of visiting the homes and farms of Quebec pickers, where they were welcomed to inspect and purchase antiques and to take part in family parties. The pickers would have warehouses stacked full of furniture, religious carvings, and statues from churches that had been closed in rural communities. Several talented carvers worked on these impressive religious items in 19th-century Quebec and earlier. Susan recalls: "You would be walking by life-size, if not larger, statues of Saint Joseph and the Virgin Mary, pews, and pulpits."

The Copeland family on a winter picking trip to Quebec, 1968.

Susan said her parents had to earn the trust and confidence of the pickers:

"There were no signs indicating that the pickers had antiques for sale. It was more through word of mouth. They would find a picker and once there was an established trusting relationship built up, then that picker would say, 'Well you should go and see so-and-so over here.' It was a matter of building relationships and trust because, you know, these people were not … they were not necessarily open. It was not that there was a subterfuge to it, but they weren't hanging signs out saying, 'Hey this is Joe's Antique's'. They were quiet about what they did. Why that was, I have no idea; they just were. So, you had to really build up a relationship and gain their trust for them to then send you on to a guy maybe ten miles down the road."

Of those winter antique buying excursions in the family's Rambler station wagon, Susan recalled:

"You know we would go to some places that were so rural that the only way you could get into the house from the road was on a skidoo. And they would come out and meet us and take us in to where they were keeping all of the furnishings and everything that they had for sale, but we had to go in over the snow. It would be like seven or eight in the morning, and they would pull out the vodka and be making pies and things like that. I had a lot of fun in Quebec."

Susan also lent a hand to her parents by helping them with set-up and take-down at antique shows. "I worked a bunch of them, like Wimodausis in Toronto. I worked that [show] with them because I was living in Toronto at the time. After I finished work, I would then show up and run the booth with them."

Display of antique items owned by Murray and Mary Copeland about 1979.

Susan recalled the strict guidelines in place for those shows. "This was a very pivotal time in the days of 'Canadiana'. I think that the first show that they ever did was at the Government Employees Market (GEM) store in Ottawa. Shows such as North Hatley and Bowmanvile and Wimodausis had such stringent pre-1867 (pre Confederation) vetting rules. My parents were very in accord with this."

Murray Copeland and a helpful dealer carry an antique cupboard into the Kingston antique show in 1977.

Well-known and long-time dealer and collector, Bill Dobson of Smiths Falls, has many memories of the Copelands. He would often meet the couple at antique shows in Ontario and Quebec. "I was selling at forty antique shows a year. I did twenty shows in Ontario and twenty in Quebec. I would continually run into Mary and Murray at those shows in Quebec."

Bill credits the Copelands for his interest in early glass: "Murray and Mary were probably two of the people that got me interested in early blown glass and porcelain." At the time, Bill had a busy antique business selling Canadian furniture."

Like many advanced collectors, the Copelands had collections within their collection featuring special areas of interest. and they would seek out some of the best examples of those items. Chief among their interests was Staffordshire earthenware pottery featuring Canadian scenes.

Also called transferware, these were pieces of china made primarily in England depicting various

Earthenware Platter, Enochwood & Sons 1830, "Polar Bear Hunting". Photo from Transferware Collectors Club, transferwarecollectorsclub.org

Davenport "Montreal" oval platter, c. 1835, printed in brown with a view of Montreal from St. Helen's Island on the centre, the steamboat 'British America' prominent in the foreground. Photo by Waddingtons.

scenes of popular landmarks in North America. In the manufacturing process, the potter used an engraving, usually done on a piece of copper, from which a monochrome print was made on paper. The print was coloured and the image transferred by pressing the engraving onto the ceramic piece. The transferred print was protected by glaze and fired in the kiln. While manufacturers tended to concentrate on American scenes, items with Canadian images were also made.

"...there will come a time when ceramic specimens showing our first steam boats, our first railways, the portraits of our distinguished statesmen, soldiers and sailors, the openings of our canals, the various events of our wars and our triumphs in peace, will rank in historical collections with the vases of Greece."

— Mary Copeland

Mrs. Copeland also wrote extensively about Canadian images on Staffordshire. One article from 1977, published in the trade newspaper *Circa 76*, carefully documents the Canadian scenes manufactured by Francis Morley and Company of Hanley, Staffordshire, between 1845 and 1858. The company used the name "Lake" on the reverse side of its pottery.

She wrote: "the ware is extremely popular with Canadian collectors as it incorporates at least ten Canadian views adapted from engravings, after drawings by W. H. Bartlett for Canadian Scenery, by N. P. Willis." She then delves into the various manufacturers' marks found on the pottery and how the company name and ownership evolved over time. Mrs. Copeland also described different models, the intensity of the glaze, and available colours.

One paragraph especially illustrates her knowledge of the subject and the history upon which a particular scene was based—including, in one case, a pertinent fact the manufacturer ignored:

"The series 'Boston Mails' introduced by J. and T. Edwards in 1841 has long been considered the province of U.S. collectors as commemorating a Trans-Atlantic Liverpool to Boston mail service. Ignored was the fact that Samuel Cunard, founder of the line, was a Haligonian and the initial contract was to link Liverpool to Halifax, Nova Scotia, with Boston as the terminus."

She also lists the Bartlett views she has seen on Morley's *Lake* products. I include a portion of that list here to demonstrate her knowledge, including a comment about a subtle detail on one of the pieces:

"Georgeville on the eastern shore of Lake Memphremagog (Quebec), Hallowell (Bay of Quinte), renamed Picton in 1847 (Ontario); 'Scene Among the Thousand Isles', picturing an Iroquois camp: 'Village of Cedars, River St. Lawrence' at the mouth of the Ottawa River (Quebec); 'The Chaudiere Bridge, Near Quebec', at the 'Rideau Canal, Bytown', looking north toward the Ottawa River; 'Church at Point-Levi' reputed by Tyrwhitt to be St. Joseph de Levis, built in 1818 (note the word 'Bethel' on the church pennant which survived the engraving to the finished product."

In 1982, for a feature article in *The Upper Canadian*, Mrs. Copeland wrote this impressive introduction:

"Later on, as our country began to have a history, the Ceramic Art began to do what it has done in all ages and civilized countries, illustrate in permanent pictures the events of history. With whatever disdain the collector of Dresden and Sevres may now look down on the blue-printed crockeries of Clews and Wood and Ridgway, there will come a time when ceramic specimens showing our first steam boats, our first railways, the portraits of our distinguished statesmen, soldiers and sailors, the openings of our canals, the various events of our wars and our triumphs in peace, will rank in historical collections with the vases of Greece."

"[The Copelands] had a particularly good eye for the form of a piece and dealt primarily in early Quebec and Georgian furniture as well as early smalls from the 18th and 19th centuries. When they came home with a particularly great find they would often give me a call. We would sit in their living room over a few drinks and discuss the merits of the piece, turning it over on its back and inspecting the tool marks, air burn and other signs of age."

– Steve Cunliffe

The Copelands were traditionalists. They liked formal furniture accented with figured maple and they purchased many fine examples in Atlantic Canada. They had no time for new trends, even if those trends later developed into serious collecting categories. Although museums, galleries, dealers, and collectors enthusiastically embraced contemporary folk art, the Copelands dismissed that out of hand. They spent their lives immersed in antiques and traditional folk art—objects that had all been created in Canada's early settlement years. How, they must have thought, could anyone get excited about folk art created by *living* artists? Where was the history in that?!

The Copelands collected, bought, and sold what they loved and knew best. Many dealers share their stubborn resistance to new fields of collecting, while others are quick to recognize the growing popularity of new categories of collecting and stock items accordingly. Yet others focus on the specialties they developed early in their careers.

In 1990, auctioneer Tim Potter sold the stock of the Copeland's Antiques plus a large portion of their personal collection. The catalogue stated:

"The collection, put together over the past 30 years, features a very large selection of flint glass in both coloured and clear, Export china, over seventy five pieces of blue on white transfer ware, a signed Rockingham tea service (1826 –1830), and a small section of quality country furnishings and over one hundred pieces of fine silver."

After Murray Copeland passed away in 2006, Mary Copeland had an auction to downsize their collection.

By 2007, both Murray and Mary Copeland had passed away and in November of that year, the balance of their personal collection was transferred to Tim Potter Auctions. This final sale featured a range of excellent items. There were Quebec cupboards in original paint; Windsor chairs from Ontario and Quebec; an outstanding two-drawer, cherry and figured-maple sideboard from Upper Woodstock, New Brunswick; trade silver; Quebec sugar moulds; and, several other excellent pieces of furniture. Most importantly, the sale included the Copeland's personal collection of Canadian and American transferware, featuring several pieces of "Arctic Scenery", which is extremely rare. After Murray Copeland passed away in 2006, Mary Copeland had an auction to downsize their collection.

After the auctioneer's hammer dropped, there was no doubt about the rarity of the transferware, especially the Arctic-themed items. The thirteen pieces of Arctic Scenery transferware alone realized a total of $26,050. The beautiful sideboard from Upper Woodstock brought a hammer price of $2,900.

This elaborate and beautiful sideboard is constructed of primarily of figured maple and cherry. The elaborate gallery with a centre fan adds a further level of sophistication to this exceptional piece of furniture. c. 1840. Now in a private collection in Ottawa.

A superb little drop leaf table in tiger maple c. 1850 was one of the lots in the Copeland's auction. It is now in a private collection in Ottawa. Photo by Marge Shackleton.

Murray and Mary Copeland each epitomized the persona of the dedicated collector. They sought out the rarest of Canadian historical objects and hunted for the best examples of a particular category, be it furniture, pottery, flint glass, silver, or traditional folk art. They did thorough research

A primitive arm chair from the Copeland collection. c. 1840. Photo by Marge Shackleton.

and their depth of knowledge enriched their lives and helped guide them toward further exciting acquisitions. They set high standards for themselves and their collections and they lived up to those standards.

While I did not know the Copelands personally, I think of them fondly every time I drive by the McMurtry General Store in March Township, and every time I see a Canadian scene on Staffordshire pottery.

Please see Appendix Three for Steve Cunliffe's full account of his memories of the Copelands.

Photo courtesy of Jennifer McKendry.

18
VISIONARIES AND THE REST OF US

If an object or work of art has true quality in its design, it will stand the test of time and be recognized for those attributes. Collecting is a big, messy, often confusing world and whether you are actively participating as a collector or dealer, you will witness the rise and fall of trends. Trends take time to establish and it takes a visionary to recognize quality and to act on the trends that will endure. The McKendrys and the Copelands recognized quality and focussed on buying the best examples they could find.

The field of antiques and folk art has had its share of visionaries. Edith Halpert (1900 – 1970) was ridiculed in 1920 when she opened a gallery in which she included modern art downstairs and traditional folk art upstairs. Among her early and longstanding supporters, she counted Abby Rockefeller (1874 – 1948), who amassed a collection of folk art purchased largely from Mrs. Halpert. Not only were Mrs. Halpert's folk art offerings deemed unworthy by many collectors, her gallery was located in the decidedly *non*-gallery SoHo area of New York City.

Shaker furniture and accessories are among the most sought-after antiques in the U.S. today, yet there was little interest in them until 1923, when Edward Andrews (1894 – 1964) and his wife, Faith Andrews (1897 –1990), began to document and collect the furniture and accessories of this declining utopian sect. The Shakers designed and constructed some of the most beautiful furniture and accessories ever made by human hands. Creating any object was, to them, akin to a religious experience. Thomas Merton (1915 – 1968), a Trappist monk and American essayist, wrote: "The peculiar grace of a Shaker chair is due to the fact that it was built by someone capable of believing that an angel might come and sit on it."

The price of some antiques and art escalates as the awareness and understanding of work by a certain artist accelerates over time. More and more people, including dealers and collectors, come to realize the significance of what a particular artist was attempting to accomplish.

I would love to own a painting by Grandma Moses, for example, but with entry level pricing on good examples running at $75,000, I am not likely to acquire one unless by accident. The same can be said for 18th-century Quebec furniture, Tiffany lamps, and Gustav Stickley furniture. The quality of these pieces is such that, over time, growing recognition drives prices up as demand increases—sometimes to a point where only collectors with the deepest pockets can afford them.

Yet, even if you cannot afford the highest quality pieces or hot trends, there is value for any collector in understanding why a Shaker harvest table can sell for $150,000, why paintings by Grandma Moses sell for $100,000, or why a Quebec antique armoire may sell for $50,000 and more. These pieces are excellent learning tools, and understanding the surface, form, condition, age, provenance, artistic expression, and other factors that make an object desirable will help you recognize greatness in an as-yet unheralded find.

Many superb collections are put together on the advice of dealers working closely with collectors who have the desire and funds to underwrite the cost. Dealers know the sources for excellent material and, more importantly, they know what makes a great piece great. Buying antiques from reputable dealers who belong to organizations like the Canadian Antique Dealers Association (CADA) can eliminate much of the uncertainty around your purchases. A dealer should work with you to find specific items for your collection. That cooperation can and should include offering you attractive payment terms for more expensive items.

Looking back on my collecting career, I wish I had bought fewer items but acquired (and kept) more of higher quality. That means, to some extent, my collection is diminished from what it might have been. Many forces come to bear on a collection, including collectors and dealers who will happily separate you from the best items you have in exchange for often irresistible amounts of money. From personal and painful experiences, I know that the money is quickly long gone but you always remember a special piece you have sold from your collection, especially if you are unable to replace it with another piece of similar or better quality.

Ottawa collector, Paul Warman (1944 – 2011), showed me his collection of country furniture and accessories—a privilege he afforded to very few people. Paul's collection was extensive, as he had acquired antiques and folk art over many decades. He told me that when he first started to collect, he showed a particularly nice antique to a dealer. Naturally, the dealer wanted to buy it, and Paul acquiesced. Soon after, he suffered seller's remorse and decided there and then he would never again sell a piece from his collection—and he did not. I have also known individuals who assembled impressive collections only to sell the lot and start over again!

Two Quebec blanket boxes that will certainly stand the test of time. They have been part of our collection for several years.

Rare is the individual who recognizes the genuine new-arts movement in the moment it begins. In your collecting career, you may never be that person—most of us are not. Most collectors take their cues from others who are already collecting certain forms. What you can be, however, is a collector who understands why certain antiques and art are desirable in whatever category you choose to collect. Examine new trends closely, as they may offer a new and interesting category of items for you to collect—or not. Train yourself to recognize quality and be prepared to pay for it, because you will never regret it.

Rare, open, shoe footed dish dresser in pine, c. 1830. Found in a country auction in West Quebec and purchased there by me in the early 1980's. Current whereabouts unknown.

19
Good, Better, Best, and Learning to Discern

The biggest challenge for every collector, especially those new to the field, is determining whether an antique is the good, better, or best of its type. (There are also levels of poor below good to be avoided). A new collector has little or no context from which to make informed decisions. Thus, many collectors start slowly and buy at the lower end of the quality range. I shudder at some of the things I bought when we first started to collect—I had enthusiasm but little else to go on. It takes years to build your knowledge base. In the beginning, you can also put your faith in reputable dealers and purchase items from them. Doing so is a solid strategy, although you will generally pay retail prices for their quality antiques and folk art.

Fortunately, I came to know a few pickers and saw what they were bringing back to their homes and shops. Joan and I began to attend country auctions in the Ottawa Valley on a regular basis. In the 1980s and into the 1990s, there were still many genuine farm auctions at which generations of material—sometimes four and five generations of accumulation—were sold. Though we did not buy much, it exposed me to the material, and I became accustomed to seeing antiques "in the rough".

Occasionally, we would arrive at an auction and no other collectors or dealers would be there. I remember a sale in Shawville, Quebec, by auctioneer Revell Stewart of Cobden, Ontario. There was not much at the sale except an extremely nice round candle stand, almost tea-table sized and completely original, including alligatored brown paint. We waited for the table to come up for sale and bought it for about $50.

I knew the little table was good; I did not know it was excellent. Not long after, my brother, Scott, and I decided to sell some things at the Stittsville Flea Market. We loaded the truck early on a Sunday morning and, at the last minute because there was still room, I ran back into the garage, picked up the candle stand and found a spot for it in the truck.

Just moments after we pulled into the flea market, found a space, and turned off the engine, the late Warren Snider (1944 – 2018) a dealer with an incredibly sharp eye for quality antiques, walked up to the truck and spied the candle table. He lifted it out and asked loudly, "How much for the table?"

I hesitated then blurted, "A hundred dollars."

"Fine," said Warren, "I'll take it."

He took out his wallet and peeled out a couple of fifty-dollar bills, quickly handed them to me, then disappeared into the crowd with the table. Thinking back on it now, the table was probably worth at least $500. New collectors and dealers often make such mistakes, and experienced dealers know to stay close to individuals just starting out because they often find extraordinary items and can underprice them.

On another occasion, I had come across one of the best harvest tables I had seen up to that point and for many years later. I was picking farms in Quebec about thirty miles north of Ottawa, stopped at an old farm, and a gentleman came to the door in the back kitchen. Even before he answered, I had spied a pine flat-to-the-wall cupboard against the far wall. I told him the purpose of my visit and for good measure I also said, "I buy antiques like that old cupboard behind you."

He invited me in to look at the cupboard and said he also wanted to show me an old table in the kitchen. We entered through the back door and there, just a few feet in front of me, was a long table covered with a flower-patterned oil cloth that hung down a good twelve inches around the entire table. It was hard to see anything of the table.

"Could I lift up the tablecloth to take a look?" I asked politely.

"Sure," the owner said, "go right ahead."

I can still remember leaning down to lift the side of that oilcloth. Underneath was a six-foot pine harvest table with a drawer in the side and, better yet, an "H" stretcher base running down the length of it that connected the tapered legs. A six-foot length in a table is important. Anything

These bear paw snowshoes are certainly the best I've ever owned or seen. They are generally attributed to the Naskapi and neighbouring tribes located in the northern boreal forest/subarctic area of Quebec and Labrador, c. 1900. Excellent, as found condition. Private collection.

less means the table is not ideal to seat three people on each side plus a single person at each end. Many larger harvest tables have been found: eight feet, ten feet, even twelve feet. Depending on form and condition, the longer ones can be very desirable, although it takes a large room to accommodate them.

Lifting the tablecloth a little higher, I was able to tell from the underside that the top was made from only two long boards, each about twenty inches in width. The only thing better than a two-board-top harvest table is a one-board top harvest table, which is extremely rare. (I've owned two in the past.)

Even as a relatively new picker and collector, I knew right away that the man's table was exceptional. Of course, he went on to say that the table and the cupboard in the summer kitchen were not for sale.

One evening several weeks later, the phone rang and it was the man with the six foot table on the line. He said he was going to have to put a new floor in the shed and kitchen which meant the table and cupboard would have to be sold. I assured him I was still interested and a few days later returned to his farm and bought both pieces.

Because they have handled or at least seen hundreds or thousands of antiques, seasoned collectors and dealers are able, with some degree of accuracy, to place a piece in their mind and compare it to the others they have encountered. This good-better-best scenario is in play regardless of what you collect. Every collecting field has its gold standard to which other items are compared and valued.

The problem for all collectors is that, in every category, less-than-good items abound. Better items are scarce, and the best items are exceedingly rare, meaning that you simply do not see or handle them much. It follows, then, that the market of buyers and sellers comes to understand over time what is scarce in a particular category and what is readily available, and prices are established based on the rarity. Other factors contribute, especially condition, but rare items in rough condition can still fetch a premium.

This places the new collector at a substantial disadvantage. It took several years before I had enough experience to gain a comparative sense of good-better-best. But a keen collector does not want to wait until they know everything—it is natural to want to forge ahead and collect. Once your interest has been piqued, you want to start collecting as soon as possible.

In some categories, such as advertising signs, the best items can be defined with some certainty. If only a handful of examples of a certain sign with great graphics are known to exist and you find another one in excellent condition, you likely have something in the "best" category. Country furniture, on the other hand, is much less definitive. While you can find "best" examples in reference books, these are not manufactured items, so your chances of finding another item exactly like those in reference books are slim. This is when judgement, experience, and knowledge come into play.

When I started collecting, I bought inexpensive pieces of late 19th- and 20th-century manufactured furniture, usually with several layers of overpaint. I continued in that way for some time until I started to notice what types of items were fetching higher prices at auction. Soon, I wanted to own and collect objects in original paint that were not manufactured but instead hand-made. While my tastes had evolved, I had yet to handle or own many higher-quality items.

That is about the time I started picking for antiques while continuing to attend country auctions in the Ottawa Valley. In time, I was successful in finding items in original condition. While I had still a great deal to learn, at least I was on the right path.

As the old saying goes, a little knowledge is a dangerous thing. With antiques, the danger is the amount of money you may spend to acquire an object based on your assessment. It can be intimidating, especially if someone else has already made an offer on the piece. The antique-collecting world is competitive—sometimes fiercely so. People will go to extraordinary lengths to acquire important pieces to resell or place in their collections. Often, the only difference between one person acquiring a piece and another person losing out is timing. When the timing is right, everything falls into place and you acquire the antique. When the timing is wrong, you may miss buying a piece by an hour, a day, a week, or a month. As a picker once said to me, "In this business, you're always working for tomorrow."

Worst is when you were at a farm or home when an antique was not for sale, yet a month or two later, it is sold to someone else. Sometimes, it is simply a case of someone offering more money than you had or perhaps a better sales pitch.

Many pickers, me included, will return to a particular farm or house every year for ten or twenty years because the owner has a particularly desirable piece. It is a rare occasion when an owner calls back and offers to sell you the antique you have been wanting. More often, such a piece is not for sale and never will be.

That was the case about twenty years ago at a house in the Westboro neighbourhood of Ottawa. I don't recall what I was there to see, but as

This pine open dish dresser I picked in Lanark County is certainly the best of its type that ever graced my collection. The small size, raised panel doors, nicely balanced cornice, beaded openings and early overpaint are all desirable features. c. 1850. Author's collection.

we walked through the house, I stopped abruptly in front of a painting on the dining room wall. It was extraordinary, easily a "best" in its category. The large oil on-canvas painting depicted a winter scene of harness racing on Mississippi Lake near Carleton Place in the 19th century. In it, a horse named *Mr. Vic* is harnessed to a sulky with a driver in a bear-skin coat manning the reins. In the background, the artist painted a race with several horses. Although I do not remember the artist's name, the painting was signed and dated. It was a stunning piece of Canadian art and of Canadian history.

I admired the painting for a minute or so and the owner told me that it had been in his family for several generations. I offered to buy it for $1,000 cash on the spot, but he was not motivated at all—the painting was a treasure meant to stay in the family.

When dealers and pickers see a piece and cannot buy it, they will frequently ask if they may tuck a business card inside a drawer or on a shelf, so that if the time comes to sell, the owner can look at the card and make that important call. My friend, Rick Huxtable, once visited a farm in the Ottawa Valley where he saw an excellent antique Germanic armoire in original condition that was made in the area about 1870. Inside the cupboard, Rick discovered five business cards of other dealers and pickers! However, Rick's timing was perfect because, on that day, the owner decided to sell the piece.

I have always been a bit of a stingy buyer, tending to shy away from higher-priced items and preferring to pick the objects myself rather than buy from a dealer. Yet, on occasion, I will step up and pay the price for something that really interests me, particularly a piece of high quality.

The one downside of paying retail prices for antiques is that you will not likely see an increase in value for some time. If circumstances cause you to sell a piece for which you have paid a premium, there is a strong chance that the resale price will fall well short of what you paid. Still, there are many situations where pieces bought at retail price are sold for an even higher price.

Most collectors can recall situations when they have paid too much—we call it being "buried" in a piece. I am buried in several pieces, but the losses I expect I will take when I do sell them are not earth-shattering. Generally, however, antiques and folk art tend to increase nicely in value over time—especially museum-quality items. The "buy and hold" method of investment works in the collecting world too.

I wish I had bought and held more frequently despite rarely having had much discretionary income to buy antiques. I like to think of Herbert and Dorothy Vogel, a couple in New York City who, during their lifetimes, assembled a large and important collection of modern art and kept it all in their four hundred and fifty square-foot apartment! Mr. Vogel worked in the post office and Mrs. Vogel worked as a librarian. They allocated one of their salaries to buying art. Their strategy was to buy directly from the artist and to buy what they liked. Many of the artists from whom they bought in the 1960s and 1970s went on to become world-famous in the fields of minimalist and conceptual art. Over the years, the Vogels amassed a collection of about twenty-five-hundred pieces they eventually donated to The National Gallery of Art in Washington, D.C.

It is nice to think of putting together a collection of the best objects your money can buy. For most of us, however, our collections will be a mixture of good, better, and best pieces. Sometimes, we hold items for purely sentimental reasons or because they are family heirlooms or an antique acquired from a friend.

Consider my most recent purchases which are, by and large, modest. In 2019, I bought folk art carvings, native decorated baskets, a pair of excellent snowshoes, rustic furniture, paintings, clocks, stoneware, several pieces of miniature furniture, and some regular pieces of country furniture. With a few exceptions, each of the items cost me less than $100; several were less than $25. In a couple of cases, I spent $250 on a single item, and one piece of furniture was $350.

I found these items in antique shops, flea markets, auctions, and a few private sales. In total, I spent about $1,500 over six months—not a lot of money in the grand scheme of things; plus, I got a big kick out of every item I purchased. Not many things in life are both affordable and give you an emotional high—for me, antiques are one such rare pleasure. I also continue to derive enjoyment from my purchases each time I walk by them.

None of the items are "museum quality" or the best of the best, except perhaps the bear-paw snowshoes. Still, I enjoy every one of these objects in my collection because they are genuine examples of what I like to collect. They have added charm, interest, and depth to my collection.

No collection will be identical to another. You are the master of yours, which should reflect your tastes, preferences, and unique eye.

Interpretation of a press back armchair as made by a Germanic cabinetmaker in the Ottawa Valley about 1900. Author's collection.

20
Country Furniture of the Ottawa Valley

In the fall of 1983, I took a position working for the County of Renfrew. Joan and I moved to Pembroke, Ontario, and lived there until the spring of 1986. Since our son "Teddy" was born there in December of 1985, Pembroke will always have a special place in our hearts and minds. As I have discovered over the years, many other people have a connection with Pembroke. With a population then of about 14,000, Pembroke gave us a taste of small city living which we quite enjoyed.

Having only started to collect in about 1980, I was still very much a newbie in the field but I was fortunate in that there were still many antiques to be found in the Ottawa Valley and in particular Renfrew County. It is not my intention in this chapter to provide a detailed analysis of furniture forms or their attribution to known cabinet makers of the era.. However, I did want to document some of my experiences and share photographs of a few of the pieces I have owned or that others have acquired and kindly let me include here.

The upper Ottawa Valley has a rich and interesting history. The Opeongo Road was opened, partially, in 1851 and was to serve as a route from the Ottawa River to Georgian Bay. As an incentive, the plan included giving plots of land along the road to settlers. Several years later about 100 miles of the road had been constructed. The better lots closer to the Town of Renfrew had already been acquired by Scottish, Irish and German settlers. Polish settlers had to make their choices roughly 60 miles to the northwest. Some of them settled in the area that was named Wilno. The communities of Golden Lake, Barry's Bay, Killaloe, Round Lake Centre, Eganville and others also attracted German and Polish settlers.

For a new antique collector, I was in an excellent time and place in Renfrew County. On most weekends, there was a country auction to attend, as well as tag sales and yard sales. It was quite common for me to run around to yard sales on a Saturday morning, fill my truck with antiques and then go to an auction the same day and buy more antiques! We also made regular visits to a small number of antique shops in the area.

Saturday farm auctions at the time were popular and well attended. A sale of a farm and all its contents could easily attract three hundred people or more. It was an opportunity for the local farmers to look over and possibly buy a new piece of equipment. It was an opportunity for dealers and collectors to discover antiques that had been stored away in the house and barns for many years. Since 19th century farms typically had a house, several barns and sheds, there were literally wagons full of material to sell including the furniture and accessories made by previous generations of the family having the auction.

Pickers have combed Renfrew County and adjacent municipalities for years, and many fascinating pieces have come to light. The pickers were certainly present and active, practically on a daily basis, during our years living in Pembroke.

Renfrew County's 19th-century craftsmen made furniture for use in their modest log houses and for the many fellow immigrants who came to settlements north west of Ottawa in search of a new and better life. Certain pieces of furniture were fundamental to the settlers' homes, such as storage cupboards, beds, cradles, blanket boxes, tables, pail stands, wall boxes, and freestanding shelving. These makers repeated the designs of furniture in their home lands, which often included unique details. Occasionally a wall box, a clock shelf or small document box that includes specialized details will turn up. These small often unique accessory pieces are rare and extremely popular with collectors.

The late Brenda Lee-Whiting (1929 – 1994) was a resident of Deep River in Renfrew County and wrote extensively on the Germanic settlements of Renfrew County. Her two books are: *Harvest of Stones* (University Press, 1985) and *On Stony Ground* (Juniper Books, 1986). In an article in the July/August issue of *Canadian Antiques Collector* magazine, Lee-Whiting pointed out the differences between furniture made by the Polish and German immigrants, and lamented that antique dealers and pickers often confused the two styles, sometimes intentionally.

This situation arose because the demand for Polish furniture and accessories from the Wilno area was, and still is, intense. Adding the word "Wilno" to a price tag can elevate the price of a piece considerably. But, as Lee-Whiting points out, Canada had more German immigrants than Polish and she refers to a ratio of six-to-one in census records throughout the 19th century. Thus, she concludes, the Polish population in Renfrew County was too small to have produced all the items in the antique market at that time. Despite this fact, many antiques from the Upper Ottawa Valley are inaccurately described as Polish or Wilno in origin.

A splint basket from Wilno dating to about 1900. Picked in 1983. Author's collection.

A pine blanket chest from the Wilno area of Renfrew County. This one shown in overpaint. About 1860. Private collection.

Despite living relatively close to Wilno, about a 45 minute drive from Pembroke, my purchases of Polish items were rather few and far between. On the few occasions I did search for antiques in the Wilno / Barry's Bay Area, I had limited success. My purchases included a nine foot pine bench in

A pine blanket chest from the Wilno area of Renfrew County and purchased from an old Ottawa collection. About 1870. Author's collection.

original colour, and a primitive splint basket both from an early Polish farm. The basket is still in my collection.

In the early 1980s I also picked a two piece cupboard in the village of Barry's Bay, however it was not Polish in design or construction. What I tended to find in the County was Germanic furniture which, as Brenda Lee-Whiting noted, was far more prevalent than furniture and accessories with a Wilno / Polish origin.

In the late 1980s, I was able to buy a Wilno blanket box from an old Ottawa collection. This box was all original with many of the distinguishing features of Wilno boxes including the front panelled construction, high scrolled base and three different colours of paint: overall blue with light green panels and red painted trim. Oddly, it does not have the floral decorations on the panels nor does it appear that the box ever had them. It too has now been in our collection for over 30 years.

The armoire, or wardrobe, form is typically a large case with two doors, sometimes a full-width drawer at the bottom, and a cornice. Armoire doors of the period typically have inset flat panels, occasionally decorated with wavy frames. Two doors are most common. Structurally, cornices were part of the case, or sometimes a wavy strip of pierced, decorative wood was fastened to its top edge. Often, these featured elaborate details and carving, usually with a central feature, such as a raised half-oval or a rectangle carved with symbols that were important to German families. Stylized sheaves of wheat, hearts, and fans are examples of the central feature the makers in-

Armoire in as-found condition, at auction. Golden Lake, Ontario. Private collection.

corporated into their cupboards. Hand-made wooden hooks embedded in a horizontal cross-piece affixed to the inside rear wall of the armoire were common, and the hooks were also made to swivel.

These furniture makers used mostly wooden pegs for joining, including wooden pins embedded in the top and bottom corners of the doors, on which the doors pivoted without the need for metal hinges.

When I purchased one such cupboard nearly 100 years after its construction, its quarter-inch wooden door pins still worked flawlessly. My piece had the rectangular feature in the cornice, but no carving. It also had the full, deep drawer at the bottom with porcelain knobs. The feet were missing but it featured its original varnish.

The armoire I purchased was constructed of pine, the most frequently used wood species for such wardrobes and other case pieces. However, some German cabinet makers in the Valley frequently used black ash. Like oak, black ash has a pronounced grain which, once varnished, really stands out. Some makers ebonized the cornice trim and corner trim, meaning they painted it black and produced a nice contrast with the varnished ash. I have also seen some terrific examples in original old red paint which, as noted earlier, was the cabinetmaker's attempt to simulate the look of mahogany.

I sold my cupboard in the late 1980s at an antique show, then saw it again fifteen years ago. It was like seeing an old friend after a long absence.

About ten years ago, on a hot July day, I drove to the village of Golden Lake to take in an auction of an old Germanic farm. The farm was accessed by a long laneway off one of the two regional roads that passed through the village. It seemed as though the pickers had missed this old farm or at least the family living there had not sold off all of the old pine furniture and other antiques that on this day were displayed on the lawns around the house and outbuildings.

Toward the end of the sale, the armoire was put up for sale. Collector Mike Brown and I bought the piece that day, but I later sold him my share. (No room at the Markey residence for another cupboard!) Although it had served as storage in an adjacent barn, the cupboard was still intact. It was made entirely of pine, square nailed, and was in early paint.

Once you have seen a few examples from Renfrew County, you will not be confused by imported European items. Renfrew County cupboards typically do not have decorative floral painting on the doors or fronts. You will most often see cast iron hinges or perhaps steel. Chamfered edges with lamb-tongue stops are common, as are small block feet often turned at an angle. The County wardrobes are wood-pinned and one often sees square-cut nails in the back, but not hand forged.

This excellent glazed cupboard in overpaint was constructed by John Kozlowski who came to the Wilno area in 1876. He left for the USA in 1903. Private collection.

Among the most interesting and alluring furniture items made by Polish and German settlers in the Ottawa Valley are flat-to-the-wall cupboards. Cupboards meant to store pottery, glassware, china and cutlery were made by most country cabinetmakers. The basic form is a case with a shelved upper portion either closed by glass doors or simply open shelves.

Germanic cupboard from Renfrew County. Pine. About 1870. Overpaint removed to first surface. Author's collection.

In my forty years of collecting in the Ottawa Valley, I have seen about six food lockers. I picked a reasonably good example in Petawawa Township in the early 1980s. True to the form, it had a single door with short, narrow slats about twelve inches in length cut through the door at about eye level. It had a cornice, stood about five feet high, and was in reasonably good condition after having sat inside the door of a barn for about seventy-five years.

I saw another example at an auction in Schwartz, a farming community a few miles north of Shawville, Quebec—another destination for German settlers to Canada in the late 19th century.

The food locker was one of many items being auctioned from an original log homestead and farm. The place had been deserted for a few years and a great-grandson of the original settlers had decided to sell off the contents of the home and outbuildings. Just about everything was there, still in situ: furniture, much of it homemade: horse-drawn equipment, sleighs, hand tools, stoneware—it was like a museum except everything there was for sale. That included tools and equipment used to extract and process white pine from the forests. Heavy chains, cross-cut saws, stone boats, stump pullers, and a myriad of cast iron hand tools were plentiful in the log barns and sheds. It was evidence of the labours and difficulties of life in those times. This farm had also operated with no electricity.

In one of the log buildings stood the pine food locker. It had a single door above an open set of shelves and the door featured an intricate grill design. Strangely, the maker had constructed the upper section quite a bit longer than the lower cupboard section. To make design matters worse, the upper section jutted out about three inches over the lower section, making the whole piece top heavy. It was overpainted in a thick coat of light blue. Still, I thought it was interesting and would have bid on it except that I was influenced by my group of friends, who dismissed it as ugly. That did not stop another picker from the Valley from stepping up and, after intense bidding, he bought the locker for $975.

Some food lockers can be found in a "pierced tin" variety. I have never seen an authentic Ontario pierced-tin food locker. They show up from time to time at local antique markets but I do not believe them to be Canadian in origin. I did see one from the Ladysmith area of west Quebec, but it was small and crudely built. If someone offers you an "Ontario" pierced-tin food locker, you can safely assume the origin, unless they have detailed provenance, is incorrect.

Stands built to hold containers of water and associated accessories are known by a few different terms: pail stands, bucket benches, and water stands. Pail stands are different from pail cupboards, which were built usually with a closed cupboard above open shelves.

Typically, the edges that face forward on the top section of the sides of pail stands are stylized with a cut-out of some sort. By design, the top of the sides and the back form a partial enclosure—a splash guard that keeps water somewhat contained to that area.

At the base, the sides are usually embellished with a simple semi-circular cut-out, or "boot jack"-type end, although I have seen many examples with the sides left square and the bottoms flush to the ground. The cut-outs are certainly more attractive.

Pail stands are difficult to find today. Most were made of pine, constantly exposed to water, and kept outside on a covered back porch beside a rear door—they lived hard lives. Many simply rotted away and their remnants were disposed of in wood stoves. Still, examples survive and collectors like them because they are functional and serve as excellent pieces of early furniture on which to display stoneware, redware, and related accessories. Personally, I have bought about a half-dozen over the years and wish I had bought more when I saw them.

The pail stand is a rudimentary form: five or six boards at the most. Two of the boards form the sides, which extend down to the floor and serve as the "feet" of the piece. For today's collector, desirability increases in proportion with any extra design features the cabinetmaker added to the basic construction.

The areas of the stand that could be embellished were limited to the top back board, the front edges of the sides, and the flat sides at the base. Occasionally, the top edge of the exposed back board is shaped with a scroll or sometimes a sawtooth-type cut out.

I vividly recall a dark-blue painted pail stand with scrolled back board and front edges at an auction near Kemptville in the early 1980s. The scroll work, combined with the early, if not original, paint made it a desirable piece of early Ontario furniture. When the stand came up on the block, two veteran dealers, the late Ray Clarke and Ken Lawless, went to battle over it. Ray took it home for a hammer price of $1,200—a serious bit of money in those days.

The best example of a pail stand in my collection is a tall, grungy, yellow piece I bought from Rick Huxtable many years ago. It has a nice form and may have been built by August Boehme of Renfrew County, as it is similar in form to one by him pictured in Brenda Lee-Whiting's book, *Harvest of Stones*. It has graduated shelves that decrease in depth from the bottom shelf to the top. Like some pail stands, the narrow top shelf would have been used to store a cup or two and a soap dish. Mine also sports a horizontal back rail or narrow splash board attached vertically to the top shelf, a considerate addition by the maker, as it would have been difficult to store items there without them frequently falling off.

A pail stand in original paint from the Wilno area, with elaborately scrolled back board and sides. Likely dates to about 1875. The scroll work elevates what would have been a rudimentary piece of furniture to something with far more design appeal. Private collection.

Today, most pail stands in paint range between $1,000 and $2,000. To go above $2,000, and occasionally they do, a pail stand needs to have a lot going for it on all counts: surface, form, condition, age, and provenance. Repairs and restoration should be at an absolute minimum and the vendor should be aware, as best they can, of what specific restoration has been done to a piece.

An interesting late 19th century washstand in ash, likely made by a Germanic cabinetmaker from the Upper Ottawa Valley. (Huxtable Antiques)

If you are on the lookout for a pail stand, take your time. Refer to the book examples and look at what is available on the market. It also follows that, at the higher prices, the dealer should provide provenance: solid information about the origin of the piece and, ideally, details about the previous owners. In the end, you will have to make a judgement call based on the information available.

As a collector of antique furniture, I am frequently looking at furniture in the back of pick up trucks. Most of what I see is for sale, and even when it is not, it is still interesting and exciting to examine a fresh load of antiques.

Two weeks ago, Rick Huxtable stopped by our house with antique furniture. One of the pieces was unusual. While common in form, a washstand in his truck exhibited characteristics that suggested the work of a Germanic cabinet maker in Renfrew County or from a farm in the Upper Ottawa Valley.

Despite losing its original surface, most likely a dark brown varnish, the stand still made a wonderful statement about the quality and sometimes quirkiness of rural furniture construction in the mid- to late-19th century.

The reverse side of the washstand's backsplash showing the creative wooden support.

Made entirely of ash, a wood favoured by Germanic cabinet makers, the most remarkable feature of the stand is the splash board that rises from the rear edge of the top and finishes in a large, stylized heart. Clearly, this back board was meant to do a serious job of preventing water from splashing on to the wall behind the stand.

The backsplash is effectively supported by a thin rectangular wooden brace twelve inches in length affixed to the centre rear apron of the stand and continuing up the reverse side of the backboard. Using only one brace in the centre created challenge for the cabinet maker: how to finish the straight top edge of the brace at the lowest centre point, the "V" of the splash board where the top of brace would be visible? Remarkably, this was achieved by whittling the top of the brace so it was smooth and even with the edge of the splash board where the two pieces meet.

Another attractive feature is the stylized front brackets supporting the simple six-sided towel bars made with a spoke shave and not turned on a lathe. The tapered, round legs exhibit the simplest of turnings, just enough to define the upper and lower portions. The cabinet maker was also careful to provide a handy lapped drawer, but the pint-sized version he included is wildly out of proportion given the size of the front board on which it is centred. Still, it is a functional drawer and spacious enough to hold soap.

The features of this washstand are why many of us collect furniture. These quirky yet elegantly functional pieces speak to us about the individuals who designed and made them. The washstand form was predetermined, yet 19th-century cabinet makers found ways to incorporate often unique

Exquisite clock shelf from the Wilno area of Renfrew County. The precise and elaborate scrolled cutout around the base of the shelf make this an outstanding example of the form. c. 1860. Private collection.

features to elevate a simple piece of furniture to something more interesting—and now appealing to collectors.

While this chapter has focused on Germanic and Polish furniture of the Ottawa Valley, furniture and accessories of this style are also found in other areas of Canada. The Kitchener-Waterloo and Markham areas of Ontario; the Lunenburg area of Nova Scotia; and, the Schwartz, Ladysmith and Poltimore communities of west Quebec were also settled, in part, by families with German ancestry. The furniture and accessories from those regions are often extraordinary in terms of their design and form. They continue to be popular with collectors.

Early Ottawa Antique Dealers, Philip and Marge Shackleton

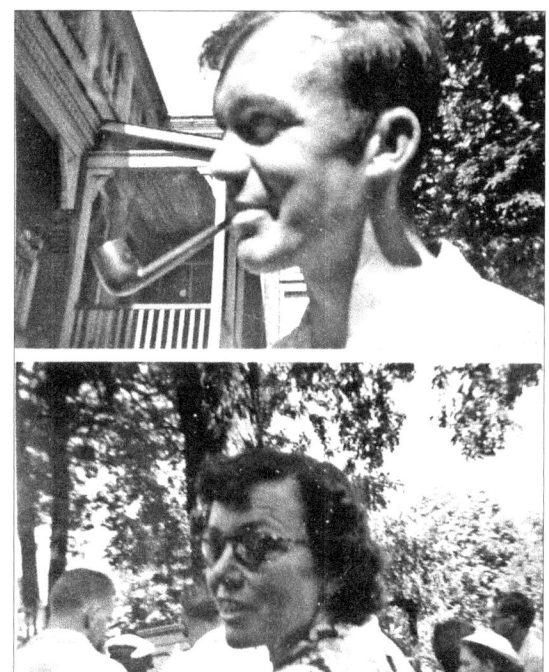

Marge and Philip Shackleton at their farm and antique shop in Manotick, Ontario, about 1965.

Philip Sutcliffe Shackleton (1923 – 2017) and Marge Shackleton (1927 – 1967) were prominent figures in the early Ottawa antiques scene. He was educated at the University of Toronto and a decorated athlete. She was an accomplished news photographer in Ottawa.

Mr. Shackleton approached Canadian material history as a scholar. He viewed antiques from a broad perspective and understood how historic events influenced the tastes and styles in furniture and accessories prevalent here in the 18th and 19th centuries. He and Mrs. Shackleton were ardent fans of Ontario antiques. In a 1976 newspaper article in *The Milton/Canadian Champion*, Mr. Shackleton is quoted as saying: "I don't collect local furniture because it is great but because it is ours."

The Shackletons were pioneering collectors of early Canadian antiques and folk art. In the early 1960s, they opened their store, The Country Shop, on Laurier Avenue. The Laurier location housed both their antique business and her photography studio. In 1963, Mrs. Shackleton founded a publication, *The Canadian Antique Dealers Directory* which she continued to research and publish for several years.

The antique business was successful to the point that it overtook the photography space. In 1965, they moved their residence and operations to a century farm on River Road near Manotick, about twenty minutes south of Ottawa. (The word "manotick" comes from the Algonquin word for "island". It was named by Moss Kent Dickinson (1829 – 1887), one of the first settlers. Prior to that the area was known as Long Island Locks, part of Colonel John By's Rideau canal system). At their Manotick farm, there was room for a large antique store and a separate space for Mrs. Shackleton's photography studio.

By this time, Marge Shackleton had shifted her career away from news photography to de-

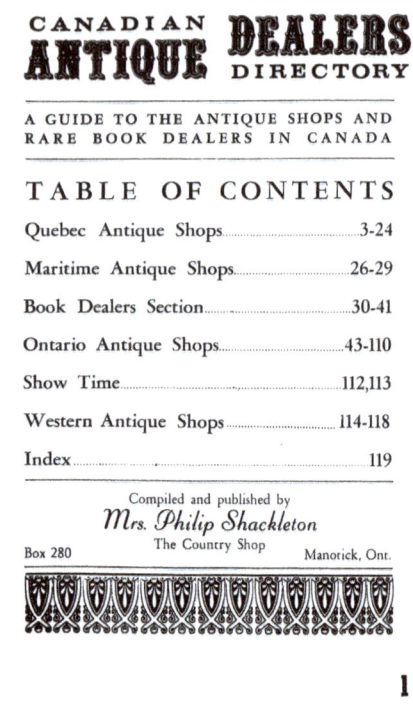

Advertisement for Marge Shackleton's directory of Canadian antique dealers, which she compiled and published in the mid 1960s.

Advertisement for the Shackletons' antique shop in 1960 on Laurier Avenue in Ottawa, Ontario.

vote herself to the photography of antiques. Their concept for a major book about Ontario antiques with text written and researched by Mr. Shackleton and several hundred photographs taken by Mrs. Shackleton had firmly taken hold by 1965. From that point on, they split their time evenly: he managed the acquisition of antiques and the shop while she devoted her time to photography. Alternating weeks would find her photographing antiques from their collection or in other collections away from home. She developed

The Dickinson Mill, Manotick, Ontario. Present day.

all her own prints and catalogued her burgeoning collection of photographs many of which were destined to become part of their ultimate project: *The Furniture of Old Ontario*.

Mr. Shackleton took exception to the word "Canadiana", believing it to be a misleading catch-all term. "There's too much vague talk of 'Canadiana' as if it were a category that suggests a style. It does not do anything of the kind," the *Milton/Canadian Champion* newspaper article quotes him as saying. "Canada's early furniture styles displayed a mixture of design trends popular at the time. English designs found their way here when cabinetmakers emigrated. The designs of Sheraton, Chippendale, Hepplewhite, Duncan Phyfe, and other influences can be seen to a lesser or greater degree in antique Ontario furniture both country and formal."

Marge Shackleton photographing an antique chair. Early 1960s.

In May of 1967, Mr. Shackleton wrote an article on early furniture for *Canadian Antiques Collector* magazine. In the article, he makes the point that the antique furniture of Ontario was not all pine and was not limited to a few forms like dough boxes, dry sinks, and arrow-back chairs: "But crudity in furnishings was by no means the frontier rule. A large number of the colony's early residents were people of wealth or taste or both. Few of them wanted packing crates in their drawing rooms."

> *"The truth is that the furniture makers of Upper Canada, just plain handymen and cabinet makers, used the finest as well as the cheapest of local woods and also whatever exotic lumber was imported and made available. You can find Ontario furniture made in everything from basswood to mahogany."*
>
> – Philip Shackleton

Mr. Shackleton also explains the major influence of United Empire Loyalists on furniture styles in Upper Canada: "The 18th century, that golden age of good design in the western world, was waning when the first refugees from the American Revolution raised their tents on the north shore of Lake Ontario. Our Ontario craft history belongs essentially to the 19th century, the period when designers were obsessed with wave after wave of revivalism."

Shackleton took exception to collectors who focus only on primitive furniture styles as if that was all that was made here in the mid-19th century. He writes:

> "There are still collectors who seem able to accept only crude design and the commonest of local woods as real evidence of Ontario production. The truth is that the furniture makers of Upper Canada, just plain handymen and cabinet makers, used the finest as well as the cheapest of local woods and also whatever exotic lumber was imported and made available. You can find Ontario furniture made in everything from basswood to mahogany."

In August of 1966, Mrs. Shackleton was interviewed by Beverly Morin for the *Ottawa Citizen* newspaper. By then, the Shackletons were deeply immersed in the research and photography for their book and their antique business continued to prosper.

In the article Mrs. Shackleton reflects on the time and effort she and her husband had put into the antiques field, and the special attention they were now putting into the book project: "We've spent the last fifteen years trying to preserve Canadian handmade furniture. Of course, we've always photographed the best pieces but now we're trying to do a really good job."

In the same article, she lamented the loss of so many Canadian antiques to the United States. "Many of the finest examples of pioneer work are in American hands—the museum in Detroit for one. And Americans flock up here to pick up what they can find."

That statement was offset by another comment about the success of their business and the rapidly growing interest in Canadian antiques: "We're riding the crest of a wave of tremendous interest in anything Canadian," she says in the article. "Business is fantastic. Maybe it's the Centennial but it seems that anything old, handmade is in demand if it's Canadian."

While the Shackletons pursued the antique business and built their own important collection of antiques, they also found the time for other antique- and heritage-related projects. Mr. Shackleton was consulted on several major initiatives, such as furnishing buildings in Upper Canada Village, Dundurn Castle, and other significant heritage sites. It was a busy and productive time for both of them.

While Mrs. Shackleton poured untold effort into the photography for the book, she would not see its completion. Tragically, she died prematurely during surgery on May 24, 1967, at just forty-two years of age.

Philip and Marge Shackleton, mid 1960's.

Their book was finally published in 1973 and launched to a highly receptive audience at the Kingston Winter Antique Show that same year. Mr. Shackleton dedicated the book to his late wife and wrote the following within it:

In Memory of Marge Shackleton

This book had its beginnings in her keen enthusiasm for the craft traditions of Canada's settlement period. The work was begun in partnership and she completed the first of the photographs, principally at Upper Canada Village and Black Creek Pioneer Village, before her death in 1967.

The Furniture of Old Ontario marked an important inflection point in the field of Canadian collecting. Other books about Canada's material history had come before the Shackletons'. A decade earlier, Jean Palardy had published his seminal book, *The Early Furniture of French Canada*. Jeanne Minhinnick had published *At Home in Upper Canada* in 1970, examining daily life in early Canadian homes, room by room, including furniture and accessories. In 1972, Scott Symons had published *Heritage: A Romantic Look at Early Canadian Furniture*.

Only the Shackletons' book, however, focused entirely on the antique furniture of Ontario of the 19th century and presented the topic in a detailed and comprehensive manner. In it, Mr. Shackleton examined all the prominent trends in furniture design at the time, including formal and country variations. The book

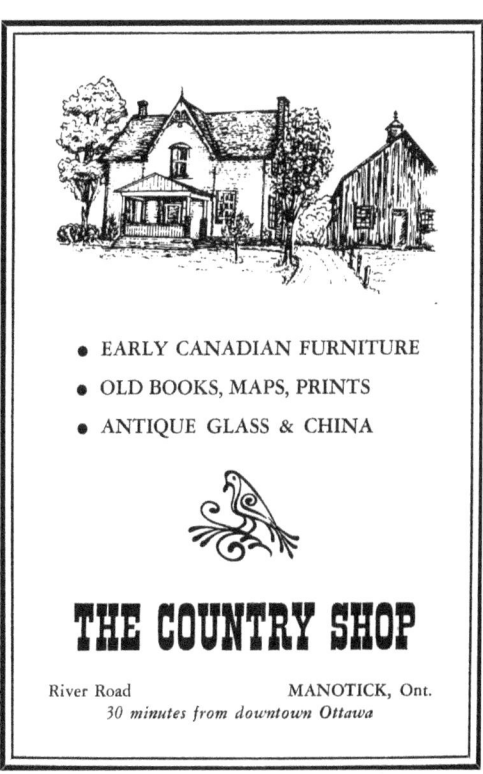

1966 advertisement of Marge and Philip Shackleton's home and antique shop in Manotick, Ontario.

Windsor chair photographed by Marge Shackleton that belonged to Murray and Mary Copeland.

resonated strongly with Ontario collectors. It, along with Howard Pain's *Heritage of Upper Canadian Furniture*, published ten years later, would become cornerstones in the libraries of nearly all collectors of early Ontario furniture and accessories.

In an interview I conducted with collector, dealer, show promotor, and publisher, Bill Dobson, he attributed the growing interest in preserving original finish on antiques to both the Shackletons' and Pain's books. "It is interesting that from Philip's book and on to Howard Pain's, there was such a shift in how we thought about leaving things as-found, as we found them or in the original finish. I give credit not just to the people who wrote the books but the dealers who started really focusing on original finish."

In 1983, Mr. Shackleton and Kenneth G. Roberts achieved another publishing milestone when they collaborated on *Canoe – History of the Craft from Panama to the Arctic*. The comprehensive book is beautifully designed

The Shackleton stamp on the back of one of their photographs.

and informative. It is as impressive as Mr. Shackleton's first book—when it came to publication projects, he left no stone unturned.

The lives of collectors often intersect, as was the case with Philip Shackleton and the document sleuth, Hugh P. MacMillan (1924 – 2012). A 1979 article in the *Ottawa Citizen* by Allan Levine describes the discovery and preservation of the papers of Hamnett Kirkes Pinhey (1784 –1857), one of the early settlers of March Township who arrived in Upper Canada around 1820. Mr. Pinhey owned land and his business interests included the operation of the Bytown and Nepean Toll Road Company. In 1822, he built a Georgian stone home named Horaceville after his eldest son, Horace. The house still sits majestically on the banks of the Ottawa River in March Township.

Mr. Shackleton was an important link in the chain of events that led to the discovery and salvation of the Pinhey papers. In 1966, he was called by an auctioneer, the late William (Bill) Walker, to examine what was left in a Pinhey family home in the Glebe neighbourhood of Ottawa. Several dealers and pickers had already been through the house and removed all the desirable antiques and art. However, as frequently happens, they left all the paper items, including letters, posters, photographs, diaries, and business records. According to the article, the house's interior was awash with such material.

Philip Shackleton unloading furniture at the Kingston Winter Antique Show, 1977.

The importance of this accumulation was not lost on the scholarly Mr. Shackleton, who helped salvage items like an important personal diary kept by Hamnett Pinhey from 1829 to 1840. Mr. Shackleton helped Mr. Mac-Millan contact Charles Hill, a great-great-grandson of Pinhey and retired curator of Canadian art at the National Gallery of Canada. With Mr. Hill's cooperation, the Pinhey papers were donated to the Archives of Ontario. This trove of important documents vividly reflects the early days of development and business in this part of the province, and its preservation was due in large part to Shackleton's quick thinking.

In November of 1986, in what was the beginning of a process to disperse the collection he and his wife had amassed, Mr. Shackleton consigned the pottery portion of their collection to Tim Potter Auction Services. It was a landmark sale and included items that must have had the grapevine buzzing with anticipation.

"As to the quality of its design, we collectors may in truth be able to say only that we prefer it to other furniture because it is our own."

– Philip Shackleton.

As the *Upper Canadian* noted in its review of the auction, "the sale highlight had to be the four thousand plus paid for the 'Dragon Jug'. The signed W. Hart pitcher, the Beech frame, the foot warmer all went to very happy buyers."

The one-gallon jug that sold for $4,100 had a blue serpent decoration on its front. The G.I. Lazier foot warmer that sold for $1,700 featured an unusual bird decoration in blue. The Rockingham glazed picture frame signed in script on the reverse, G. Beech, Brantford, Canada West, brought $1,600. A six-gallon Skinner & Co., Canada West open crock with two facing bluebirds above a stylized nest brought $2,000. While these items were top lots, there were also many other desirable pieces in the collection.

Three years later, in the 1988 January/February issue of the *Upper Canadian*, there was a further article about the final auction sale of items from the Shackletons' stock and personal collection. Again, collectors came out in force to compete for pieces that once formed important parts of the Shackleton collection.

The McKendrys, the Copelands, and the Shackletons were instrumental in recognizing the importance of Canadian cultural material at a time when it was far from popular to do so. They also assembled important collections and sold important pieces into collections that preserved hundreds and thousands of items.

It is difficult to be a pioneer in any new field. The knowledge, excitement, and sheer joy that Philip and Marge Shackleton took from their pursuits surely made their inevitable sacrifices worthwhile. They were passionate and had the character and unwavering dedication to discover, document, educate, and preserve early Canadian antiques, pottery, and folk art.

22
COVID-19 AND THE ANTIQUE COLLECTOR

The COVID-19 pandemic has turned our lives upside down. Those of us who can are doing what we have been asked: staying home. For Joan and I, our social interaction has been limited to outdoor visits with neighbours and our son and daughter-in-law—physically distanced and bittersweet. We are learning how to use FaceTime and Zoom with comically mixed results.

Being largely confined to our house and yard every day for months has given me plenty of time to reflect on how important antique and folk art collecting is to our lives. I know this pastime is far down the list of priorities from protecting health and saving lives. Still, there are many things I miss about collecting and, frankly, I now realize I took a great deal of it for granted.

Collecting reaches into many corners of one's life. I miss dropping into our local antique market to look at the offerings, to chat and joke with friends and dealers about what they have acquired or what they are chasing. These days, we are quick to bring out our cell phones and scroll through photos of the antiques and folk art we have seen recently but have not, as yet, been able to buy. Our conversations are full of hope and wishful thinking that these acquisitions will come sooner than later.

I miss trips to flea markets, where I would arrive at daybreak in hopes of finding something special. I miss road trips to antique stores in the smaller towns outside the city. I miss the sense of anticipation when opening the doors and venturing into those shops.

I miss country auctions on summer days, which meant the chance to visit a farm that perhaps the antique pickers had missed or where they had run into a stubborn farmer who would never sell the old pine cupboard in the shed. Often, the desired cupboard was not there or we would be outbid, but the morning air was cool and fresh, the people were friendly, and the home-baked apple pie sold from the kitchen was still warm from the church-ladies' ovens.

I miss occasionally picking for antiques and folk art on my own, the (mostly) friendly greetings, and a walk out to a drive-shed where the owner said there were old things up on the second level I could investigate.

I miss my collector friends and their collections of antiques and art. Every collection is unique, and to be with a collector in their collection is a joy and a privilege.

Most of all, I miss bringing home a new antique or piece of folk art and the thrill of placing the object in its new surroundings, where it will hopefully bring pleasure for many more years.

Life has changed so much. We all yearn for a normal time when we can resume the lives we were living—including collecting and preserving the material history of Canada.

Read More about Shaun Markey's Antique Adventures!

For more stories about antique and folk art hunting, order Shaun Markey's first book: *Folk Art in the Attic*.

Written in 2015, Shaun's first book includes chapters about many more searches for antiques and folk art. While most were successful, Shaun also includes interesting often humorous episodes about the antiques and folk art that escaped his grasp. Like the second book, the first volume includes information and advice on how to build an antique collection.

Order *Folk Art in the Attic* today and have the two of the most comprehensive books about antique and folk art collecting in your library!

Purchase your copy of Folk Art in the Attic or additional copies of Antique Memories from: www.shaunmarkey.ca

Photo courtesy of the *Ottawa Citizen*.

Epilogue

Life lived is memories and this book reflects a good number of them since my first book in 2015. I am so fortunate to have had an adult life filled with the enjoyment and excitement that collecting antiques and art can bring. I've shared the pleasure with my wife, Joan Markey and many friends, old and new, who I've come to know across Canada.

Several collector friends have passed away in the last five years and that's been a great loss to us and everyone who knew and loved them.

The passion for antiques and folk art is a common and resilient bond between collectors. This is especially true in the last year since the COVID-19 pandemic changed our lives so dramatically.

If you're not a collector, I hope this book illustrates something of the enjoyment that comes with collecting not just antiques and folk art, but *all* antiques and art. If you are a collector, I hope this book held your interest, passed along useful information, and occasionally brought a smile to your face.

I hope, finally, that the book has properly recognized the important individuals who came before us. The McKendrys, the Copelands and the Shackletons, among others, discovered and carefully documented literally thousands of significant Canadian antiques and folk art. They laid a strong foundation for the collectors who came later. Their research, books, articles, photographs, and legacy of passing on knowledge have made us better collectors, better antique sleuths, and better custodians of Canada's material history.

Acknowledgements

This book would not have been possible without the support and cooperation of so many people.

I want to thank my wife, Joan Markey, who had the patience and good spirit to listen to my endless ramblings about the content of the book. When my spirit for the project waned, as it frequently did, Joan was always encouraging and supportive. She frequently sent me back to my desk with renewed energy and commitment for the project.

Jennifer McKendry was gracious and patient in answering my questions about her parents, whom I unfortunately never met. She embraced the project from the outset although she did not know me, a stranger calling from Ottawa who wanted to write about her parents. Jennifer quickly responded to all my emails, talked to me on the telephone, and allowed me to use several family photographs. Jennifer also provided the photographs and images for use in the chapter about Phillip and Marge Shackleton and the photograph on page 152 introducing Chapter 18.

Susan Copeland was also enthusiastic and helpful, both during a lengthy telephone interview about her parents' involvement with antiques, and in providing family photographs for use in the book. Susan was moved by the fact that I wanted to write about her parents and I hope the chapter on their fascinating careers in antiques lives up to her expectations.

Steve and Sue Cunliffe knew the early dealers in Ottawa and were unfailingly helpful in providing me pertinent background information, including the first edition of the *Upper Canadian* and several issues of *Canadian Antiques Collector* magazine, such as the first edition from the spring of 1966 and several other issues from that year. Steve was enthusiastic about this project and gave me full access to his extensive library of books, papers, and photographs. For example, in 1964, Philip Shackleton compiled a directory of potters in 19th-century Ontario for the then National and Historic Parks Branch of the federal Department of Indian Affairs and Northern Development. I had never heard of it, let alone seen it, yet Steve had a copy! His knowledge of Canadian antiques is deep and he was always willing to share that knowledge with me.

Bill Dobson of Montague House Antiques provided assistance and enthusiasm that was integral to this book. Bill's memory of times past is legendary, and he was generous to a fault in sharing that knowledge with me.

Rick Huxtable of Richard Huxtable Antiques has been a friend since we first met at an auction in the Ottawa Valley in 1981. He has picked some of the finest antiques and folk art to come out of the area and has helped me in all my projects. He guested on my television series, provided photographs, or allowed me to take photographs of relevant items in his collection for this book, and has lent his support to other media projects of mine.

Gavin Wilson of Gavin Wilson Antiques arranged my interview with the late Patrick "Pat" Patterson of Renfrew, the son of Abe Patterson. Gavin also permitted me to take photographs of carvings by Abe Patterson in his collection and provided several anecdotes that I incorporated into the book. I am sorry that Pat passed away before I finished this book.

Claude Arsenault endured many emails and messages from me. At my request, he hunted through boxes and files to come up with several fascinating photos of his career in antiques and folk art. To this day, Claude is a passionate advocate for Canadian material history and contributes to the heritage preservation of buildings and the early cultural objects of Prince Edward Island.

Dr. Alvin "Nick" Cameron graciously permitted me to use his definition of folk art. Nick's attention to detail and unwavering interest in Canadian antiques and folk art is infectious. Nick and his wife, Carol Cameron, have supported all my projects, not the least of which included transporting beautiful and important examples from their collection to the Rogers TV studio for my series about antiques and folk art.

Jon Church is a good friend and fellow collector with an appreciation and deep knowledge of Ottawa history. Jon kindly allowed me to photograph pieces of his stoneware collection. It was Jon's friend David Truemner, who conducted helpful research on Marge Shackleton that I put to good use in the book. Jon also joined me for several front-porch and back-deck visits throughout the summer and autumn of 2020 to chat about antiques and folk art. Those visits helped both of us get through the long, drawn-out seasons of the pandemic.

Carol Telfer has always been helpful during my writing projects. Thank you Carol for your input on the Grenfell Mission chapter.

Alison Stalker of Ruth Stalker Antiques helped me with research in the early stages of the book. A visit to Ruth Stalker Antiques, owned and operated by Alison and her brother Jamie in Montreal, Quebec, is always a terrific experience.

Ken Aubrey of Aubrey Antiques provided me with fascinating stories about antique and nostalgia collecting. Ken was enthusiastic about my first book and kept copies for sale in his store. He also guested on my television show.

Bill Kendall provided useful background information about the early days of antique collecting in Quebec.

The late Hugh Gough, certainly one of the best pickers I have met and an expert in the early furniture of Prince Edward Island, was kind enough to provide me with some exceptional photographs that added context and a touch of humour to the book.

Mike Brown kindly provided photographs of important Renfrew County items in his collection.

Now in a private collection, the photo of the Wilno pail stand on page 177 was kindly provided by Pridham's Auction House Inc.

Suzanne Herrick-Lee and Steve Lee welcomed me to their home to take photos of Wilno furniture in their collection.

Ernie Johnson of Ernest Johnson Antiques has been continually supportive of my various projects, including this book, and I thank him for his ongoing support.

Thank you to Herb and Sophie Bond, who frequently published my articles in their *Canadian Antiques & Vintage* magazine.

I am grateful to Jack Craft of Finer Things Antiques, who provided the photographs of the John Tulles table and a portion of the Olsen collection. Jack was always supportive of my media relations work for the Canadian Antique Dealers Association (CADA), of which he is an active member.

Christopher McCreery, Executive Director of Government House in Halifax, NS also provided me with a photo of the Tulles table and I appreciate him doing so.

Thank you to Cynthia Randell, Manager, Grenfell Historic Properties, St. Anthony, Newfoundland Labrador, for providing the photograph of Dr. Wilfred Grenfell used in Chapter 4.

Louise Henderson and Tyler Shouldice provided important information about John F. Shouldice and Jenny Shouldice for use in Chapter 15.

Mark Wilson answered my Facebook call for back-issues of *Canadian Antiques Collector* magazine. In fact, Mark gave me his collection of the magazines, which included all issues from the years of 1967 through 1970. The very first one I opened, May 1967, contained the article "Upper Canadian Furniture" by Philip Shackleton with photos by Marge Shackleton, which I quoted from in Chapter 21.

When I mentioned the possibility of this book, several individuals were steadfastly enthusiastic and encouraged me to proceed with the project. I specifically want to mention: Bill Dobson, Robin Ritchie, Jon Church, Pierre Menard, Chris Spick, Rick Huxtable, Moe Johnson, and Gavin Wilson for their encouragement.

Don Hewson has been a supporter of mine for several years. He helped me with my television series and is always promoting my abilities as a publicist.

Scott Markey assisted with a great many digital scans of old photographs and printed material which I subsequently used in this book.

Matt Zambonin gave me full access and use of photographs he took of my collection for *Folk Art in the Attic* some of which also appear in this book. Matt is an excellent photographer. http://mattzamboninphoto.com

Maria Ford deserves so much credit for tackling the job of editing the manuscript. I value Maria's sharp eye, clear thinking, and critical evaluation of the overall book.

Todd Coopee of Sonderho Press was patient and supportive while guiding me through the independent publishing process from beginning to end.

The design of the book is the talented work of Denis Savoie, also of Sonderho Press. As with my first book, Denis made this one beautiful throughout.

Barbara Lukaszewicz took on the arduous task of proof reading the final manuscript and did a thorough job of it. Many thanks Barbara!

Appendix 1

When the National Gallery of Canada, of which Joan and I are members, made plans to sell a significant piece of art by Marc Chagall to raise money to acquire Jacques-Louis David's "Jerome Heard the Trumpets of the Last Judgment", the story gained considerable traction in the media, including national outlets. I took the opportunity to write a letter to the editor of the Ottawa Citizen newspaper about the proposed transaction. Much to my surprise, the paper published it. Because it is relatively short, I include it here:

~

Re: Gallery mystery solved, April 12, 2018

The real mystery as to why the National Gallery is flogging an impressive painting by Marc Chagall to free up funds for a work by Jacques-Louis David is not the identity of the work they're chasing (now confirmed); it is why our country's major art institution is reduced to selling off one major asset to buy another.

An annual budget of $8 million for acquisitions strikes me as inadequate for a national organization. Have a look at the prices worldwide for significant pieces of art by well-known artists. I am all for frugal government spending but I am also an arts supporter.

More importantly, it is not like the gallery is "spending" the money and it is gone! This is not a multi-million-dollar spend on a consulting study or technology that will be out of date in two or three years. The gallery is gaining an important asset on behalf of Canadians and, surprise, assets like these paintings "go up in value over time."

Shouldn't there be a special policy in place for situations like these, when gallery executives could make a detailed recommendation to the federal government for funds to cover one-time, unique purchases? Simply giving the gallery money on an annual basis and saying "Here, you figure out what to do but don't ask for more" may be a reasonable fiscal decision but it shows a complete lack of understanding of the art market. It also chains the gallery to an arbitrary budget figure that looks good on the surface but in all likelihood severely limits its acquisitions ability.

Give the gallery the resources, on all fronts, to seriously act like a national institution. Let it be known to the art world at large that Canadians take their art seriously and have the resources and mandate to act when the time and the opportunity arises.

Appendix 2

While working on publicity for the Canadian Antique Dealers Association (CADA), I canvased the members for interesting stories about antiques. Jack Craft of Finer Things Antiques in Halifax, Nova Scotia, replied with a story revolving around a dying collector's final wishes about a famous little table and what would happen to it after he passed away. This is the story I wrote about it:

~

Halifax Collector's Final Wish – Donate Rare 19th Century Antique to the People of Nova Scotia

Jack Craft of Finer Things Antiques & Curios in Halifax was not sure what to expect when he was summoned to the hospital bed of local collector, Reidar David Olsen, who was gravely ill. As it turned out, the collector wanted Craft's help to disperse his superb collection of antique furniture, the majority of which was made in Atlantic Canada. In particular, he was most concerned about an exquisite two drawer Sheraton stand attributed to 19th-century Halifax cabinet maker, John Tulles (1771 – 1827). Craft appraised the table at $10,000.

"It was a collection that was put together over many years and had several excellent 19th-century pieces in it," said Craft. "It was the dying wish of Mr. Olsen who placed his collection with me so that I could find the best possible home for the Tulles table."

It did not take long for Craft to land on the idea of offering the table as a donation to Government House in Halifax. Government House is one of the oldest consecutively occupied government residences, and one of the oldest such official residences in North America.

He contacted the Executive Director, Christopher McCreery, who immediately expressed interest in the piece and arrangements were made for the table to be donated. "I was pleased to see the table stay here in Halifax and in a setting where everyone can see this terrific example of Tulles' work," said Craft.

Craft recently recalled how he first crossed paths with Reidar Olsen. "I had known who David was for 20 plus years although he did not know me. I had seen him at local auctions and would always marvel at his discerning eye—he only bought the best of the best. After I opened my store 15 years ago, he became a customer and we struck up a good rapport. It was not too long before we realized we had very similar tastes across many categories, and over the past five years he became one of my most valued customers."

For Nova Scotia, John Tulles is considered the best furniture maker of his time. In fact, other experts have stated that he was the finest Canadian furniture maker of the early 19th century. Little is known about the man. Ross Fox of the Royal Ontario Museum, in research for an article on Tulles' furniture, was able to ascertain that he was born on December 26, 1771 in Ferryport-on-Craig (now known as Tayport) in Scotland.

Reidar Olsen's father was from Norway and served in that country's merchant navy during WWII. His father met his mother, a resident of Mahone Bay, Nova Scotia, around that time, and they ended up marrying and settling in Nova Scotia. Shortly after, David was born. Although his name was Reidar, everyone knew him as David.

Craft also commented on Mr. Olsen's passion for Canadian antiques. "He took an interesting approach to buying because his interests spanned from 18th century to mid 20th century, but his greatest loves were 19th-century Nova Scotia furniture and mid-20th-century maritime Canadian studio pottery, and the two seemed to work well together in a decorative setting."

Reidar Olsen had no children and collecting was his true passion. He and his partner would attend auctions together and travel the countryside visiting antique shops and estate sales. He enjoyed the research as much as the collecting. When his home was cleaned out there were volumes of reference books, magazines, and other periodicals related to the antiques trade stacked from floor to ceiling. He was a true scholar.

The two-drawer table is attributed to Tulles based on several distinct features, particularly the inlays, found in his works. In the Sheraton style, it dates to about 1815. The main carcass is constructed of bird's-eye maple with a two-drawer configuration comprising a single drawer over one larger deep drawer faux-fronted to appear as two separate drawers. The cross-banded top is in mahogany. The tapered legs are string-and-dot inlaid and terminate in brass caps and casters. Identical inlays have been found on labeled pieces of Tulles furniture and documented in the book, *Heritage Furnishings of Atlantic Canada: A Visual Survey with Pertinent Points* by Henry and Barbara Dobson. The Royal Ontario Museum in Toronto has three pieces of furniture in their collection attributed to Tulles.

I also wrote a news release from the story about the Tulles table and distributed it to the media. This led to excellent coverage in Atlantic Canada, including a feature article in the *Halifax Chronicle Herald*. The article brought exposure to CADA, to Jack Craft, and to Canadian antiques in general.

Appendix 3

As I was doing the research for Chapter 15, Steve Cunliffe shared an unpublished piece he wrote, titled "Remembering the Copelands". With his permission, a slightly edited version is reprinted here:

~

I first met Mary Copeland some forty years ago while in my late teens. I roared up on my Triumph motorcycle to the Copeland antiques shop in South March just outside of Ottawa. When I entered, I found myself, as author and antique expert Scot Symons would say, "in my first cathedral experience". There sat Mary at an Ontario cherry drop-leaf table surrounded by various worktables, chests of drawers and other furniture in tiger maple, cherry and butternut; and yet other pieces in pine all finished in the ubiquitous golden or pumpkin pine that was popular at the time.

I had always been interested in antiques but had really no knowledge. A few years later, when my wife, Sue, and I started looking for furniture for our apartment, we visited the Copeland's shop on a more regular basis, since at that time antiques were less expensive than new furniture. The two half-round serving tables from Prescott, Ontario in butternut and maple in the centre of the shop which we walked around and around with our first son on my back became our kitchen table. We still have the table.

Murray and Mary Copeland began antique collecting and dealing shortly after finishing their university studies in the mid 1950s. Their first antique was a comfortable American Boston type rocking chair that was refinished, but which they always kept in their collection.

The Copelands began by selling antiques on Saturday afternoons out of their wooden garage located on Hare Avenue in Ottawa's Glabar Park neighbourhood. Like most antiques from that era, the furniture was frequently stripped of original finishes with the use of caustic chemicals. Furniture was then sanded to remove the furry surface wood fibres that resulted from the stripping process. At the time, the Copelands stripped and refinished most of their finds but did retain painted surfaces if original and pristine. They did not, however, sand the daylights out of the surface, as many others did, so their pieces always had an impressive aged look.

Murray tried his best to educate us on the finer points of antique furniture. I remember he was particularly disappointed when he could not persuade us of the merits of a mahogany sofa with "hairy paw" feet acquired on the St. Lawrence riverfront. At that time, there was a choice of tiger maple work tables at $35 to $65. We would turn our noses up and leave those that had too many ring stains on the top!

Mary did the furniture stripping of their latest finds behind the garage in their exceptionally large treed backyard. Murray did minor repairs and applied the finishes on furniture. Many different concoctions of stain were tried. Later, it became known that orange shellac was often used back in the day as a finish and thus became the gold standard among antique dealers.

Visitors to the Copeland home were surprised to see that they had several antique Quebec cupboards in original paint and other furniture in original finish.

In these early years there were no books on Canadian antiques apart from a slim guide to all types of Canadian antiques written by Gerald Stevens and a book about the antique silver of Quebec. Mary's American background provided them with information on style influences and, like other dealers, they relied on American publications, such as Wallace Nutting's three-volume set, *Furniture Treasury, and Field Guide to American Furniture* by Thomas Ormsbee. Early on in our friendship, Murray gave me a dog-eared copy of the latter.

The Copelands bought and sold locally, at first making house calls and visiting second-hand shops in the Ottawa and St. Lawrence Valley regions. Murray was a paleontologist, and his field work took them to Quebec and Atlantic Canada.

I often helped Murray load and offload for the shows and when they arrived home from their buying trips throughout Ontario, Quebec, the Eastern Townships, and the Maritimes. They had a particularly good eye for the form of a piece and dealt primarily in early Quebec and Georgian furniture, as well as early smalls from the 18th and 19th centuries. When they came home with a particularly great find, they would often give me a call. We would sit in their living room over a few drinks and discuss the merits of the piece, turning it over on its back and inspecting the tool marks, air burn, and other signs of age.

There seemed to be an endless supply of Canadian patterned glass and kerosene lamps in the Copeland's shop. When one rare piece was sold, it was immediately replaced with another. Mary would later recount how they would buy the glass on their trips literally filling the truck with boxes full of glass. Mary was an early member of GlassFax, an association formed by collectors and dealers with an interest in Canadian glass.

The Copelands collected and sold early Canadiana items and had no interest in later antiques such as decoys, stoneware, and folk art. They did collect traditional folk art and had several extraordinary pieces in their collection, including a large, malevolent looking rooster weather vane from an early chapel in Louiseville, Quebec. It dated to the early 18th century and occupied a prominent place atop an early Quebec armoire in their kitchen. The piece was later featured on the cover of *'twas ever thus, A Selection of Eastern Canadian Folk Art*, a companion publication to an exhibit of the Price collection of folk art at The Robert McLaughlin Gallery in Oshawa, Ontario, in 1979.

Around this time, "painted furniture", original and otherwise, became the popular choice with the Mckendrys, Copelands, Shackletons and, by this time, Tim Potter as well. The better antique shows actually had policies limiting the sale of pumpkin pine country furniture.

At the time, there was little interest in furniture and finishes with original surfaces utilizing the show woods like cherry, figured maple, butternut, birch, and walnut, since most often the finishes had darkened over time and obscured the original beauty of the wood. This topic of discussion is still ongoing among collectors. It was not until many years later that furniture with figured wood became desirable to collectors. Henry and Barbara Dobson, in their book, *Heritage Furnishings of Atlantic Canada* (Quarry Press, 2010), would argue that where a valuable show wood such as mahogany with maple string inlay is totally obscured by black dirt and oxidation that the piece should be carefully refinished so that the show woods are visible as originally intended. They acknowledge, however, that where the finish has turned a nut-brown colour, it should be left alone.

Collectors were becoming keenly aware of early Canadian furniture in original paint and willing to go to extreme lengths to acquire an exceptional piece. As an example, I recall a time the Copelands were away on a buying trip through the Maritimes and Quebec. When they arrived home late one Sunday night there was a truck with Quebec plates parked on the side of the road. The anxious collector had been waiting hours for them to arrive. He had earlier discovered the Copelands had acquired an extremely rare armchair and he immediately set off after them, retracing the route of their picking trip to try to catch up with them. In the dark of the night, the chair was unloaded from Murray's blue Chevrolet Suburban, examined by the collector, and a deal made on the spot. The collector and the chair disappeared into the night on the journey back into a Quebec collection.

By the early 1980s, the Copelands had decided to concentrate on selling Canadian scenes on Staffordshire china, Canadian silver, trade silver, early blue and white earthenware china, hand-forged iron work, early American glass, and other smalls. They continued with the shows in Kingston, Bowmanville, and Elora. Shortly after Murray's retirement, they decided to further scale back their antique pastime. Mary was pleasantly surprised when she learned she and Murray were acknowledged in Nigel and Donna Hutchins book on Canadian Symbols, *The Maple Leaf Forever*.

In later years, after Murray had retired from the Canadian Geological Survey, they began to scale down their massive collection and inventory, beginning in 1990 with a two-day auction by Tim Potter at the City Hall in Kingston, Ontario.

That first Copeland auction included many rare smalls, such as original canoe cups and miniature Canadian pottery, blown glass, and many pieces of Canadian scenes on Staffordshire pottery. All these items were eagerly snapped up by collectors and dealers.

A second auction was required after Murray passed away and Mary needed to scale down the collection even further. Tim Potter billed the auction "Phil Shackleton and Friends" because Shackleton had sent some of the remaining things from his collection. In my opinion, the event should have been billed as "Copeland and Friends" because Mary's things outnumbered all others.

This auction featured antique furniture, including beds, chests of drawers from Nova Scotia, an early and unusual linen press of English Canadian derivation, and an outstanding but extremely simple flame birch corner cupboard from the Maritimes in original finish.

Subsequently, with Tim Potter's assistance, Mary Copeland moved to a condominium where she set up all her best antiques. A year later, on July 4—so fitting for an American—she passed away.

The third and final estate auction featured the best items of the Copeland Collection. Everything offered was of great quality and prices reflected this. The auction results were published in the Upper Canadian.

Murray and Mary Copeland imparted their knowledge freely and in doing so positively influenced many collectors. They sold numerous pieces to our national museums. Their daughter, Susan, carried out her parent's wishes, and at the single-day auction of the pared down collection, we were able to view for the last time the many early things which we had admired over the years. The auction, which was extensively advertised by Tim Potter, was well attended by dealers and collectors—the "cognoscenti"—as Mary would say. Many pieces were hotly contested. Mary and Murray would have been satisfied that the fruits of their years of collecting went back into the marketplace to be enjoyed by others. We are greatly honoured to have known such good friends and antique dealers.

BIBLIOGRAPHY

Books

Field, Richard Henning, *Spirit of Nova Scotia, Traditional Decorative Folk Art 1780 – 1930*. Art Gallery of Nova Scotia, Halifax, NS / Dundurn Press Limited, Toronto, ON. 1985.

Genest, Bernard. *Une Monde Peuplé D'Animaux, Wilfrid Richard et les siens, sculpteurs*. Musée de la Civilisation, Ottawa, ON. 1986.

Grotz, George. *The Furniture Doctor*. Doubleday, Garden City, New York. 1962.

Laverty, Paula. *Silk Stocking Mats, Hooked Mats of the Grenfell Mission*. McGill—Queen's University Press, Montreal, PQ and Kingston, ON. 2005.

Lee-Whiting, Brenda. *Harvest of Stones, The German Settlement in Renfrew County*. University of Toronto Press, Toronto, ON. 1985.

Lee-Whiting, Brenda. *On Stony Ground*. Juniper Books, Renfrew, ON. 1986.

Markey, Shaun. *Folk Art in the Attic*. Sonderho Press, Ottawa, ON. 2015.

McKendry, Blake. *A Dictionary of Folk Artists in Canada from the 17th Century to the Present with Inclusions of Popular Portrait, Topographical, Genre, Religious, and Decorative Artists of the 17th, 18th, and 19th Centuries*. Published by Blake McKendry, Kingston, ON. 1988.

McKendry, Blake. *Folk Art, Primitive and Naïve Art in Canada*. Methuen Publications, Agincourt, ON. 1983.

McKendry, Blake. *The A to Z of Canadian Art, Artist & Art Terms*. Published by Blake McKendry, Kingston, ON. 1997 & 2001.

McKendry, Blake. *Key Dates in Canadian Art (with Jennifer McKendry)*. Published by Blake McKendry, Kingston, ON. 2001.

McKendry, Ruth. *Classic Quilts*. Key Porter Books. 1988.

McKendry, Ruth. *Quilts and Other Bed Coverings in the Canadian Tradition*. Van Nostrand Reinhold, Toronto, ON. 1979.

Minhinnick, Jeanne. *At Home in Upper Canada*. illustration design and drawings by John Richmond, Clarke. Irwin & Company. Toronto, ON, and Vancouver, BC. 1970/1983.

Morin, Beverly. "Camera Stalks Canadiana", *Ottawa Citizen*, August 17. 1966.

Nutting, Wallace. *Furniture Treasury*. 1948.

Ormsbee, Thomas. *The Field Guide to American Furniture*. 1951.

Price, Ralph and Patricia. *'twas ever thus, A Selection of Eastern Canadian Folk Art*. M. F. Feheley Publishers. 1979.

Ontario Showcase. Ontario Showcase Publishing Company Limited. Ridgetown, Ontario, page 85.

Pain, Howard. *The Heritage of Upper Canadian Furniture: A Study in the Survival of Formal and Vernacular Styles from Britain, America and Europe, 1780 – 1900*. Toronto, ON. Van Nostrand Rheinhold, Lt. 1978.

Rowan, Michael & Fleming, John. *Canadian Folk Art to 1950*. The University of Alberta Press, Edmonton, AB and Canadian Museum of Civilization, Gatineau, PQ. 2012.

Shackleton, Philip. *The Furniture of Old Ontario*. MacMillan of Canada, Toronto, ON. 1973.

Shackleton, Philip & Kenneth G. Roberts. *Canoe – History of the Craft from Panama to the Arctic*. MacMillan, Toronto, ON. 1983.

Stewart, Don R. *A Guide to Pre-Confederation Furniture of Pre-Confederation Furniture of English Canada*. Longman's Canada Limited, Don Mills, ON. 1967

Magazine, Newspaper Articles and Advertisements

Copeland Antiques advertisement. *Canadian Antiques Collector*, September / October 1979, page 70.

Copeland, Mary. *Circa 76, A Journal of Antiques and Art in Canada*. Volume 1, No. 11, 1977.

Field, Richard. *Canadian Antiques and Art Review*. July / August 1980.

Lee-Whiting, Brenda, Mistaken Identity, "Wilno" furniture suffers identity crisis", *Canadian Antiques Collector, July / August 1986. Pages 52 - 55*.

Levine, Allan. *Ottawa Citizen*, 1979.

Markey, Shaun "Gallery mystery solved", *Ottawa Citizen*, Letter to the Editor. April 12, 2018.

Shackleton, Philip, and Marge Shackleton (Photos). "Furniture of Upper Canada". *Canadian Antiques Collector*, May, 1967, pages 6-8.

Advertisement. Marge and Philip Shackleton's home and antique shop in Manotick, ON. 1966.

Webster, Donald Blake. "Canadian Georgian Furniture". *Canadian Antiques Collector*, November/December 1979. M. F. Goldenberg, Toronto, Ontario, page 28.

Wills, James T. "Tunis Snook Farm". *Canadian Arts and Antiques*. Volume 1, Number 5. February 1980. Pages 18 - 24. Halifax, Nova Scotia

Web Sites

Beswick, Aaron. Halifax Chronicle Herald. "Stand donated to Government House built by 19th century craftsman". January 2, 2019: https://www.saltwire.com/nova-scotia/news/local/stand-donated-to-government-house-built-by-19th-century-craftsman-272594/

Globe and Mail. Favourite Room, "How to mix and match antiques". Kristina Ljubanovic. Published February 14, 2019, Updated February 25, 2019: https://www.theglobeandmail.com/life/home-and-design/article-favourite-room-an-exercise-in-antique-collecting/

Globe and Mail. Favourite Room. "A historic Georgian manor outside Toronto blends a storied past with a fresh look". Gayle MacDonald. Published February 26, 2020: https://www.theglobeandmail.com/life/home-and-design/article-favourite-room-a-historic-georgian-manor-outside-toronto-blends-a/

The Lyle House: http://thelylehouse.claudearsenault.net/

Index

Andrews, Edward 153
Andrews, Faith 53
Arsenault, Claude 34-35, 38, 201
Aubrey, Ken 60, 202
Bailey, Fred 99-101
Belisle, Odessa 111-112
Billard, Dennis 61
Bond, Herbert 202
Bond, Sophie 202
By, Colonel John 184
Cameron, Carol 4, 201
Cameron, Dr. Alvin "Nick" 18, 201
Cameron, Stevie 77
Chatigny, Edmond 36, 45
Church, Jon 201, 203
Clarke, Ray 176
Colle, Sharon 127
Copeland, Mary 3, 141, 148, 150
Copeland, Murray 141, 145
Copeland, Susan 4, 200
Covey Sharpe, Nettie 79
Craft, Jack 42, 202, 206
Cunliffe, Steve 3, 141, 146, 151, 200

Cunliffe, Sue	4, 200
De Niverville, Louis	35
Desmeules, Georges	36
Dickenson, Moss Kent	184
Dixon, Art	22-23
Dobson, Barbara	46, 201, 211
Dobson, Bill	4, 76, 145, 190, 203
Dobson, Henry	208, 211
Dupuis, Hosanna	36
Ferguson, Bruce	54
Field, Richard	33
Field, Richard Henning	23
Findlay, Nora	99
Fleming, John A.	23, 114, 115
Foster, Larry	33, 92
Fox, Ross	207
Garland, Laurin	56
Gray, Herb	33
Greer, Clifton	71
Grenfell, Dr. Wilfred	21, 25-27, 31
Halpert, Edith	76, 153
Hart, William	192
Haslam, Joel	99, 108
Hayes, Brian	103-108
Hayes, Jack	103
Hayes, John	103
Hayes, Yvonne	103
Henderson, Linda	137
Henderson, Louise	203
Hewson, Don	60, 203
Hill, Charles	192
Howard, Sydney	36

Hughes, E. J. 103, 107-108
Hutchins, Donna 212
Hutchins, Nigel 212
Huxtable, Rick 44, 99, 122-123, 163, 177, 179, 201
Hynes, Linda 78
Jones, Agnes Hasey 20
Jones, Louis C. 20
Johnson, Ernest 202
Johnson, Moe 203
Kuralek, William 108
Lambert, David 40
Lambert, Nancy 40
Lambert, Robert 40
Lawless, Ken 138, 176
Lee-Whiting, Brenda 169, 177, 214, 216
Levesque, Felicien 36
Levine, Allen 191, 216
Levitin, Arthur 60
Lewis, Maud 19-20, 53, 71-72, 113, 115
Little, Nina Fletcher 76
Lumsden, Gavin 59
MacMillan, Hugh 191-192
Markey, Joan 199, 200
McCreery, Christopher 47, 202, 207
McKendry, Blake 3, 73-75, 77, 79, 81-82
McKendry, Jennifer 4, 76, 79-80
McKendry, Ruth 3, 75-77, 81, 84-85
Menard, Pierre 92, 203
Merton, Thomas 153
Miller and Miller Auctions 36
Miskelly, Jason 69
Moore Robin 30, 108

Morin, Beverly	187, 215
Moses, "Grandma"	154
Norris, Joe	19, 153, 115
Nutting, Wallace	76, 210, 215
Osler, Dr. Martin	36
Ormsbee, Thomas	210, 215
Pain, Howard	190
Palardy, Jean	189
Patterson, Abe	16, 88, 93-98, 201
Patterson, Patrick "Pat"	93, 97, 201
Pinhey, Hamnett	191-192
Pethic Cliff	40
Potter, Tim	83-84, 148-149, 192, 211-212
Price, Dr. Ralph	20-21
Price, Patricia	20-21
Reidar, David Olsen	46-47, 206-207
Reiser Force, Juliana	76
Rentz, Ewald	33-35
Richard, Damasse	44
Richard, Wilfrid	29, 32, 36-37, 39, 44
Rizner, Fred	57-58
Ritchie, Robin	203
Roberts, Kenneth G.	190, 215
Rockefeller, Abby	76, 153
Rowan, Michael J.	23, 114-115, 215
Rumi, Richard	58
Sauvé, Arthur	17, 113, 115
Schwarz, Dr. Herbert	79
Sewell, John	58
Shackleton, Marge	3, 141, 150-151, 183-193
Shackleton, Philip	84, 141, 183-193
Shakespeare, Mel	40

Shouldice, Jessie Muriel 131-133
Shouldice, Jenny 203
Shouldice, John F. 131-132, 203
Shouldice, Tyler 131-132, 203
Sleep, Joe 19, 53-54
Snider, Warren 158
Snook, Tunis 80
Spick, Chris 203
St. Germaine, Alcide 36
Stewart, Revell 157
Stuart, Sam 33-34, 65-66
Tanner, Charlie 36-37
Telfer, Carol 29, 84, 202
Tinline, Adrian 99
Tremblay, George Edward 21
Truemner, David 201
Tulles, John 46-47, 202, 206-207
Vogel, Dorothy 164
Vogel, Herbert 164
Vollrath, Chad 87, 89, 92
Vollrath, Charles 87-90 92-93
Vollrath, Glenn 92
Walker, William 191
Warman, Paul 155
Webb, Electra Havermeyer 76
Webb, James Watson 76
Webster, Donald Blake 136-216
Weston, Garfield 94
Wills, James T. 81, 216
Wilson, Gavin 94, 201, 203
Wilson, Mark 203

www.ingramcontent.com/pod-product-compliance
Lightning Source LLC
Chambersburg PA
CBHW061745070526
44585CB00025B/2810